THE TRINITY

Roger E. Olson & Christopher A. Hall

WILLIAM B. EERDMANS PUBLISHING COMPANY
GRAND RAPIDS, MICHIGAN / CAMBRIDGE, U.K.

Wm. B. Eerdmans Publishing Co.
255 Jefferson Ave. S.E., Grand Rapids, Michigan 49503 /
P.O. Box 163, Cambridge CB3 9PU U.K.

Printed in the United States of America

06 05 04 03   7 6 5 4 3 2

Library of Congress Cataloging-in-Publication Data

Olson, Roger E.
The Trinity / Roger Olson & Christopher Hall.
p.   cm. — (Guides to theology)
Includes bibliographical references and index.
ISBN 0-8028-4827-3 (pbk. : alk. paper)
1. Trinity — History of doctrines.
I. Hall, Christopher A. (Christopher Alan), 1950-   II. Title.   III. Series.
BT111.3.O47   2002
231'.044 — dc21

2001058453

www.eerdmans.com

THE TRINITY

GUIDES TO THEOLOGY

Sponsored by the Christian Theological Research Fellowship

EDITORS

Sally Bruyneel • *University of Durham*

Alan G. Padgett • *Luther Seminary*

David A. S. Fergusson • *University of Edinburgh*

Iain R. Torrance • *University of Aberdeen*

Systematic theology is undergoing a renaissance. Conferences, journal articles, and books give witness to the growing vitality of the discipline. The Christian Theological Research Fellowship is one sign of this development. To stimulate further study and inquiry into Christian doctrine, we are sponsoring, with the William B. Eerdmans Publishing Company, a series of readable and brief introductions to theology.

This series of Guides to Theology is written primarily with students in mind. We also hope that pastors, church leaders, and theologians will find them to be useful introductions to the field. Our aim is to provide a brief introduction to the chosen field, followed by an annotated bibliography of important works, which should serve as an entrée to the topic. The books in this series will be of two kinds. Some volumes, like *The Trinity,* will cover standard theological *loci.* Other volumes will be devoted to various modern approaches to Christian theology as a whole, such as feminist theology or liberation theology. The authors and editors alike pray that these works will help further the faithful study of Christian theology in our time.

Visit our Web page at
http://apu.edu/CTRF

Dedicated with gratitude
to our theology professors
Thomas Oden
and
Samuel Mikolaski

Contents

Introducing the Trinity

A Brief Introduction to the Doctrine of the Trinity

According to the church father Augustine anyone who denies the Trinity is in danger of losing her salvation, but anyone who tries to understand the Trinity is in danger of losing her mind. Many students in doctrinal classes will sympathize with the sentiment of the second half of the great Augustine's dilemma. For many Christians the doctrine of the Trinity has seemed an esoteric belief — beyond comprehension and possibly merely speculative. One wag has called it "cosmic numerology" and compared it with astrology and other occult "sciences." Even more conservative Christians often wonder whether Augustine and other church fathers and theologians have gone too far in asserting the importance of the doctrine of the Trinity. Can it really be so intrinsically connected with the gospel of salvation that denying it (not merely failing fully to understand it) results in loss of salvation or at least loss of status as a Christian? It is understandable that the importance placed on this doctrine is perplexing to many lay Christians and students. Nowhere is it clearly and unequivocally stated in Scripture. (See, however, the brief summary of the biblical basis for the doctrine of the Trinity in this volume.) How can it be so important if it is not explicitly stated in Scripture?

Twentieth-century Swiss theologian Emil Brunner was correct in averring that the doctrine of the Trinity is at least a "defensive doctrine."[1] It

---

1. Emil Brunner, *The Christian Doctrine of God: Dogmatics,* vol. 1, trans. Olive Wyon (London: Lutterworth Press, 1949), p. 206.

may not be clearly communicated in original divine revelation, but it is so clearly implied by all that Scripture says and by the logic of the incarnation of God in Jesus Christ that it is a necessary implication of and protective concept of the Christian gospel itself. To think about all that divine revelation says about God — including the sending of God's Son Jesus Christ and the unity of God as "one God" and the mission of the Holy Spirit in the world and the church — is to be forced in the direction of the doctrine of the Trinity. And one arrives at that doctrine as soon as one realizes the flaws in all non-trinitarian accounts of God.

The early church fathers of the second through the fourth centuries realized this gradually as they encountered opponents of Christianity such as the anti-Christian orator and philosopher Celsus.[2] They found it necessary to invent terms such as *trinitas* (Trinity) and *homoousios* (of the same substance) to describe the relationship between the Father and his Son — the Logos (Word) — when confronted with heretics who denied the deity of Jesus Christ and the personhood of the Holy Spirit. Heresy is the mother of orthodoxy. The doctrine of the Trinity developed gradually after the completion of the New Testament in the heat of controversy, but the church fathers who developed it believed they were simply exegeting divine revelation and not at all speculating or inventing new ideas.

The full-blown doctrine of the Trinity was spelled out in the fourth century at two great ecumenical (universal) councils: Nicea (325 A.D.) and Constantinople (381 A.D.). For over fifty years the Arian and Semi-Arian controversies raged among Christians in the Roman Empire. The various Arian groups affirmed the deity of the Father, but refused to acknowledge that the Son who became Jesus Christ was fully equal with God the Father. They were strict monotheists, even though at times they made concessions to belief in the incarnation. At the same time other Christians affirmed the full and true deity of the Son of God Jesus Christ, but rejected any true ontological distinctness between the Father, the Son, and the Holy Spirit. These Sabellians or Modalists reduced the persons of the Trinity to mere manifestations or modes of the one person God.

Against these monarchian attempts to explain away the genuine

2. Celsus, *On the True Doctrine: A Discourse Against the Christians,* trans. R. Joseph Hoffmann (Oxford & New York: Oxford University Press, 1987). Writing in the second century, Celsus refers to the Trinity as the Christians' "central doctrine" and argues against it. See p. 94.

threeness of God, the early church fathers and bishops developed language that seems esoteric to many ordinary Christians. They said that God is one *ousia* and three *hypostases* — one being or substance (sharing essential qualities equally) and three subsistences or persons (distinct in relations over against one another as well as distinct in missions in relation to the world). Any rejection of this basic trinitarian insight and affirmation (which lay behind and informed the Nicene Creed) necessarily amounts to an affirmation of some other belief about God and Jesus Christ and the Holy Spirit. Is Jesus God? Is he all of God? Is the Holy Spirit personal or an impersonal force or power? Is the Holy Spirit equal with the Father and the Son? These questions all relate to the drama of salvation and therefore they relate to what people believe about the gospel itself. The Christian gospel is that God came among people in Jesus Christ — "Immanuel" — "God with us." It also includes the unity of God: "Hear O Israel, the Lord our God is one Lord." It also includes the presence of God within his people: the Spirit indwelling and empowering Christians. This basic account of the trinitarian structure of salvation is the "stuff" of which the doctrine of the Trinity is made.

To be sure, at times trinitarian theology has taken flights of speculative fancy and lost any solid connection with salvation and Christian worship, devotion, and discipleship. But in the whole and in the main the doctrine of the Trinity has always been affirmed and defended by Eastern Orthodox, Roman Catholic, and Protestant Christians as the uniquely identifying concept of God in Christianity because it is rooted in and necessary to the reality of salvation and implied by the logic of divine revelation. The speculative flights of fancy that have sometimes led trinitarian theologians to attempt to trace the movements of the inner-trinitarian fellowship of Father, Son, and Holy Spirit in eternity apart from the world have been at best reverent attempts at "faith seeking understanding" and at worst prideful projects of "thinking God's thoughts after him."

Yet there is need for a distinction between the "immanent Trinity" (beyond the world) and the "economic Trinity" (within history) at least in thought in order to preserve the sheer gratuity of grace. If God is not already within himself in all eternity all that he essentially is and will ever be, and if God becomes what he is — triune — only in relation to the world, then the world becomes part of God's being. Saving the world, then, becomes God's self-salvation as well. In order to preserve and protect the freedom of God and the graciousness of salvation, trinitarian theologians have posited an immanence of triunity in God himself before and apart from the world. Karl Barth, the twentieth-century catalyst of a renaissance in the doctrine of the Trinity, summed it up best:

> Where the reality is there must also be the corresponding possibility. In other words, if God is "he who loves in freedom," and if God is truly who he is among us in Jesus Christ and the Holy Spirit, and if God's salvation is completely free and gracious: then the triunity of Father, Son and Holy Spirit — embedded in the very fabric of that historical reality — must also be a reality in God's own inner being in eternity.[3]

Christians who have taken the time and expended the effort to attempt to understand the doctrine of the Trinity have often, if not always, found much more in this seemingly esoteric and irrelevant doctrine than at first meets the eye. Brunner was correct that it is a defensive concept — developed to guard the gospel from distortions. But he was wrong if he thought it was only that. There is a beauty in the concept of the Trinity itself that points toward the beauty of God himself. It is the beauty of love reflected in a truth: God is love. Whom did he love before there was a world? Himself — within the fellowship of three mutually loving persons. The Trinity thus becomes a model of creaturely love and fellowship.[4] In the end, it is not an esoteric idea but a supremely practical doctrine for the guidance of Christian life and thought.

Select Bibliography of Introductions and Anthologies

Ayers, Lewis, ed. *The Trinity: Classic and Contemporary Readings.* New York: Blackwell, 2000.

Davis, Stephen T., David Kendall, Gerald O'Collins, eds. *The Trinity: An Interdisciplinary Symposium on the Trinity.* New York: Oxford University Press, 2000.

---

3. Karl Barth, *The Doctrine of God, Church Dogmatics,* II/1, trans. T. H. L. Parker et al. (Edinburgh: T. & T. Clark, 1957), pp. 326-27.

4. Leonardo Boff, *Trinity and Society,* trans. Paul Burns (Maryknoll, N.Y.: Orbis Books, 1988).

de Margerie, S.J., Bertrand. *The Christian Trinity in History.* Translated by Edmund J. Fortman. Still River, Mass.: St. Bede's Publications, 1982.

Fortman, Edmund J. *The Triune God: A Historical Study of the Doctrine of the Trinity.* London: Hutchinson & Co., 1972.

Hill, William J. *The Three-Personed God: The Trinity as a Mystery of Salvation.* Washington, D.C.: The Catholic University of America Press, 1982.

O'Collins, Gerald. *The Tripersonal God: Understanding and Interpreting the Trinity.* New York: Paulist Press, 1999.

Toon, Peter, and James D. Spiceland, eds. *One God in Trinity: An Analysis of the Primary Dogma of Christianity.* Westchester, Ill.: Cornerstone Books, 1980.

2. The Trinity in the Bible

Apart from the biblical testimony rooted in the history of salvation itself, the church as it developed would have had little motivation, need, or desire to develop a trinitarian model of God. Although there is no written word "Trinity" in the Bible, there is evidence that the concept is biblically supported in the Old Testament. In Old Testament literature, a number of concepts prove to be especially important in nudging the early Christian community in a trinitarian direction: God as "Father," "Wisdom," "Word," and "Spirit."[5] Subsequently, the New Testament church's experience of Jesus Christ and the Holy Spirit demanded a crystallization of these terms into a concise trinitarian doctrine of God.

God is referred to as "Father" relatively infrequently in the Old Testament, a total of some twenty times.[6] When the term does occur, it is often, if not invariably, related to God's covenantal relationship with Israel. God chose Israel as the people through whom he would accomplish his redemptive purposes. Despite Israel's frequent failures and sins, God as Israel's "Father" remained faithful to his covenant people.

"Wisdom," "Word," and "Spirit" sometimes function synonymously in the Old Testament, though one can observe interesting distinctions be-

---

5. Gerald O'Collins, *The Tripersonal God: Understanding and Interpreting the Trinity* (New York: Paulist Press, 1999), pp. 12, 23. We are particularly indebted to O'Collins in this short introductory essay.

6. O'Collins, *The Tripersonal God,* p. 14.

tween the three. All three terms are "vivid personifications . . . *both* identified with God and the divine activity *and* distinguished from God. . . ."[7] All three are "personified agents of divine activity . . . not yet formally recognized as persons," but operating "with personal characteristics."[8]

"Wisdom" is described in Proverbs 8:22-31 as "created" by God "at the beginning of his work" (v. 22). It existed before "the beginning of the earth" (v. 23), "before the mountains had been shaped" (v. 25), and at the establishment of the heavens (v. 27). What kind of wisdom is this? It is a wisdom intimately connected to God and yet separate from God, begotten before the beginning, delighting God and rejoicing in God and in God's creation. Biblical texts such as these served as seeds that blossomed into surprising new species in continuity with Old Testament expectations, and especially when watered by the reality of Christ's birth, ministry, death, resurrection, and ascension.

In the Old Testament, God's Word is always active, powerful, and creative. It frequently accomplishes the unexpected. It is by God's Word that creation occurs, in all its diversity and complexity (Gen. 1, Ps. 33:8-9). Often "Word" and "Spirit" function synonymously (Ps. 33:6).[9] Additionally, "Spirit" (Heb. *ruach*; Gk. *pneuma*) occurs over 400 times in the Old Testament as a "third way of articulating the creative, revelatory, and redemptive activity of God" (cf. Gen. 1:2).[10]

There is no mention of the word "Trinity" in the New Testament. What we do discover from the New Testament writers, though, is a consistent argument for the filial uniqueness of Jesus Christ in relationship to the Father of the old covenant.

Matthew plants the theme of Immanuel, "God with us" as conceived by the Spirit, early in his narrative, and he signals the distinct filial relationship between Jesus and God. Matthew closes his gospel along the same lines, as Jesus commands his disciples to baptize "in the name of the Father, Son, and Holy Spirit," which is, perhaps, the clearest trinitarian baptismal formula in the New Testament. Lastly, Jesus reminds his disciples *he will be with them*, "even to the end of the age" (Matt. 28:20). Thus, Matthew's gospel can be viewed as his narration of God's presence with Israel in Jesus.

---

7. O'Collins, *The Tripersonal God*, p. 34.
8. O'Collins, *The Tripersonal God*, p. 23.
9. O'Collins, *The Tripersonal God*, p. 31.
10. O'Collins, *The Tripersonal God*, pp. 31-32.

It is in Jesus, "God with us," that the Son is revealed and the Father through him. Indeed, all things have been "handed over" by the Father to the Son. "No one knows the Son except the Father, and no one knows the Father except the Son and anyone to whom the Son chooses to reveal him" (Matt. 11:27). As Gerald O'Collins comments, "This is to affirm a unique mutual knowledge and relationship of Jesus precisely as *the Son* to the Father, a mutual relationship out of which Jesus reveals, not a previously unknown God, but the God whom he alone knows fully and really. A distinctively new feature in Father/Son talk has emerged here."[11]

Mark does not contain the narrative of the virgin birth. Instead, Mark inaugurates the unfolding of Jesus' identity by focusing upon his baptism by John the Baptist (Mark 1:11). In a few short verses Mark teaches that Jesus' person and ministry are continuous with the Hebrew scripture's prophetic tradition and expectation, and that Jesus possesses a unique relationship with both God (the Father) and the Spirit. The question, of course, remains as to the nature of this filial relationship.

New Testament writers such as the apostle John insist that the incarnate Christ is actually the *logos* of God, present with God at the beginning and now entering the world joined to human nature (John 1:1, 14). How could the *logos* become a human being? John wisely does not attempt to explain how such could be the case. Apart from the events of the gospel narrative itself, John would never have pictured God in such a complex manner. Yet, precisely because of those events and their accompanying teaching, John insists on the incarnation of the pre-existent Son. Finally, John writes that it is through the pre-existent *logos* that creation itself has taken place (John 1:3).

Paul and the writer of Hebrews will also argue for the Son's pre-existence, but without using John's *logos* terminology. Paul writes of the Son as "the image of the invisible God, the first-born over all creation. For by him all things were created . . ." (Col. 1:15-16).[12] The writer of Hebrews speaks of

---

11. O'Collins, *The Tripersonal God*, p. 43.

12. Paul also is "redefining . . . Jewish monotheism" with his emphasis on Christ as the "agent of creation." "To be the agent of eschatological salvation (that is, of God's final kingdom) was equivalent to being the agent of the new creation (2 Cor. 5:17, Gal. 6.15). Now, what held true at the end must be true also at the beginning; eschatological claims about Christ led quickly to protological claims or claims about 'first things,' namely, that he was involved in the divine act of creation." Note also Paul's use of "Wisdom" to describe Christ, recalling our earlier discussion of the OT use of "Wisdom" in creation (1 Cor. 1:17–2:13). Paul

the Son as the agent through whom God "created the worlds. He is the reflection of God's glory and the exact imprint of God's being . . ." (Heb. 1:2-3).

Why would Paul, John, and the writer to the Hebrews propose such a strange, seemingly incomprehensible model for God, one in which "God" is "with God" while remaining a single unity? One can only point to their encounter with Christ for the answer. In short, Christ's resurrection forced them to extrude a new model of the surprisingly complex God of Israel.

We find that the New Testament writers are not only unified in their insistence that Jesus had been resurrected from the dead, but they also emphasize that Jesus' resurrection confirms his special filial status as God's Son. Jesus' prayers to God as *Abba* had strongly hinted at this unique filial relationship (cf. Mark 14:36). Paul recognized that Christ's resurrection was an undeniable vindication of "the powerful coming of the divine reign and the infinite mercy of *Abba* . . . when Jesus received radically new, indestructible life from God and with God (e.g., Rom. 6:9-10; Acts 13:34)."[13] The covenantal language of Old Testament writers concerning the Father now "moves from the margins of Jewish faith and piety to the center and will enjoy a continued and even enhanced centrality in Christian language about God."[14] Questions will inevitably emerge in light of the Father's action in raising Jesus from the dead. "Was/Is he a *divine* individual, on a par with YHWH whom he had called and addressed as *Abba?*"[15]

The early church's use of "Lord" *(kurios)* in referring to the resurrected Christ is an especially important indicator of the Son's unique filial status. Jesus, the resurrected *kurios,* "is Lord of all and is generous to all who call on him" (Rom. 10:12). Future theological debates will center on the very questions *kurios* language inevitably engenders. "Who is Jesus with his cosmic authority and what is his relationship to God the Father?"[16]

---

emphasizes in 1 Corinthians the role of Jesus as divine Wisdom "in creation (1 Cor. 8:6) and in preexistent, saving activity for the chosen people (1 Cor. 10:4)" (O'Collins, *The Tripersonal God,* p. 57).

13. O'Collins, *The Tripersonal God,* p. 51.

14. O'Collins, *The Tripersonal God,* p. 53.

15. O'Collins, *The Tripersonal God,* p. 54.

16. O'Collins, *The Tripersonal God,* p. 55. Note also that for Paul the "day of the LORD" is appropriated for Jesus. He is Lord of space, time, and history. "Paul and other NT writers took the doomsday term and reapplied it to Christ's parousia or final coming (1 Thess. 5:2), 'the day of our Lord Jesus Christ' (1 Cor. 1:8, 5:5, 2 Cor. 1:14, Phil. 1:6, 1:10, 2:16). The day of

As for the Spirit, the question was reversed. "The Spirit, being the Spirit of God, was obviously divine. But were/are we dealing with a distinct, divine individual or person?"[17] New Testament writers closely associate the Holy Spirit with both the person and work of Christ. The Spirit "overshadows" Mary (Luke 1:35). At Jesus' baptism by John, the Holy Spirit descends upon Jesus in the form of a dove, inaugurating and empowering his public ministry (Luke 3:22). The Spirit leads or drives Jesus into the wilderness to be tempted by the devil (Luke 4:1). Jesus announces in Nazareth that he is the promised one upon whom the Spirit rests (Luke 4:16).

John's gospel particularly focuses upon Jesus' relationship with the Holy Spirit in the farewell discourse (John 14–17). Jesus will ask the Father and he will give to the disciples "another" Advocate who will be "the Spirit of truth" (14:17). Jesus will not leave the disciples "orphaned," but will come to them by means of the Spirit (14:18). When the Holy Spirit comes, whom "the Father will send in my name," he will teach the disciples "everything, and remind you of all that I have said to you" (14:26). The Father sends the Spirit, as does the Son (15:26). It is actually a good thing that the Son is leaving, because when he goes he will send the Spirit to the disciples (16:7). The Spirit will glorify the Son (16:14).

Paul, too, is extremely interested in the relationship between the Son and the Holy Spirit. Paul speaks of the giving or sending of the Spirit by God, or of receiving the Spirit, but is generally not more specific in terms of who sends the Spirit. How does Paul view the individuality and personal identity of the Spirit? His verbs show him speaking of the Spirit in both an impersonal and personal manner ("poured," Rom. 5:5; "down payment," 2 Cor. 1:22; "interceding," Rom. 8:26-27; "distributing" gifts, 1 Cor. 12:11).[18] "In summary, the language of Paul's letters implies that the Spirit is a personal subject who engages in personal activities."[19]

The New Testament writers' encounter with the risen Christ and the Holy Spirit forced them to develop a theology that expanded their concept

---

God's final and decisive intervention in judgment was understood to be identified with the day of Christ's final and decisive intervention in judgment. The Lord Jesus Christ was to carry out the future function of God. The expectation of doomsday associated God and Christ to the point of their being interchangeable" (pp. 58-59).

17. O'Collins, *The Tripersonal God*, p. 54.
18. Cf. O'Collins, *The Tripersonal God*, p. 64.
19. O'Collins, *The Tripersonal God*, p. 64.

of God in an unexpected yet seemingly inevitable way. "Father," "Word," and "Wisdom" were not inconsequential characteristics of a paternal deity but rather a foretelling of a present and future relationship with God and his covenant people. Therefore we find that the God of salvation is not only one, but also three, unified in the inner relations of Father, Son, and Holy Spirit. The biblical God is Triune.

Select Bibliography — The Trinity in the Bible

Barrett, C. K. *The Holy Spirit and the Gospel Tradition.* London: SPCK, 1947.

Brown, Raymond E. *An Introduction to New Testament Christology.* New York: Paulist, 1994.

Burge, Gary M. *The Anointed Community: The Holy Spirit in the Johannine Tradition.* Grand Rapids: Eerdmans, 1987.

Cullmann, Oscar. *The Christology of the New Testament.* London: SCM, 1959.

Davey, J. E. *The Jesus of St. John: Historical and Christological Studies in the Fourth Gospel.* London: Lutterworth, 1958.

Dunn, J. D. G. *Jesus and the Spirit.* Philadelphia: Westminster, 1975.

———. *Christology in the Making.* Philadelphia: Westminster, 1980.

———. *The Parting of the Ways between Christianity and Judaism, and Their Significance for the Character of Christianity.* Philadelphia: Trinity, 1991.

Gruenler, Royce G. *The Trinity in the Gospel of John: A Thematic Commentary on the Fourth Gospel.* Grand Rapids: Eerdmans, 1986.

Harris, Murray J. *Jesus as God: The New Testament Use of Theos in Reference to Jesus.* Grand Rapids: Baker, 1992.

Hurtado, Larry W. *One God, One Lord: Early Christian Devotion and Ancient Jewish Monotheism.* Philadelphia: Fortress, 1988.

Kramer, W. *Christ, Lord, Son of God.* London: SCM, 1966.

Mettinger, Tryggve N. D. *In Search of God: The Meaning and Message of the Everlasting Names.* Philadelphia: Fortress, 1988.

Montague, George T. *The Holy Spirit: Growth of a Biblical Tradition.* New York: Paulist, 1976.

Moule, C. F. D. "The New Testament and the Doctrine of the Trinity," *The Expository Times* 78, no. 1 (October 1976): 16-21.

O'Collins, Gerald. *The Tripersonal God: Understanding and Interpreting the Trinity.* New York: Paulist, 1999.

Ramsey, Michael. *Holy Spirit: A Biblical Study*. London: SPCK, 1977.

Schaberg, J. *The Father, the Son and the Holy Spirit: The Triadic Phrase in Matthew 28:19b*. Chico, Calif.: Scholars, 1982.

Schweizer, Eduard. *Spirit of God: Bible Key Words*. London: A. & C. Black, 1960.

Swete, H. B., *The Holy Spirit in the New Testament*. London: Macmillan, 1909.

Toon, Peter. *Our Triune God: A Biblical Portrayal of the Trinity*. Wheaton: Victor Books, 1996.

Wainwright, Arthur W. *The Trinity in the New Testament*. London: SPCK, 1975.

Warfield, B. B. "The Biblical Doctrine of the Trinity." In *Biblical and Theological Studies*. Philadelphia: Presbyterian and Reformed, 1968.

THE HISTORICAL DEVELOPMENT
OF THE DOCTRINE OF THE TRINITY

1. The Trinity: Patristic Contributions

An introduction to the doctrine of the Trinity can begin in many ways. We have chosen a historical introduction, for we feel that the history of this doctrine is essential to any responsible contemporary understanding of the church's teaching on this topic. We begin at the beginning with the early Christian theologians.

Patristic trinitarian theology is grounded in a number of significant foundations. First and foremost among these is the Scripture itself, both the Hebrew scriptures and the collection of documents now known as the New Testament. In addition, early liturgies, short creedal statements, worship practices, and the overarching rule of faith of the early church provided resources and guidelines for key church fathers as they contemplated the reality of God as revealed in Jesus Christ. Both the practices and documents of the church finally led early Christian leaders to propose a trinitarian model of God, but the formation of this model took place over many years and in many contexts. As the Christian community worshiped, studied, prayed, and meditated it increasingly realized that the God whom it encountered in Jesus Christ was mysterious and complex in a manner that defied human comprehension and linguistic analysis. The conclusion of the church, reached in ecumenical council toward the end of the fourth century CE, was that God must exist as both a unity and a trinity.

Fourth-century theologians such as Athanasius argued that the Scripture, the practice of the church in worship, and the drama of salvation itself demonstrated the necessity for a trinitarian view of God. Athanasius, Basil the Great, and Gregory of Nazianzus were one in their contention

15

that biblical exegesis practiced within the womb of the church inevitably led to the need for a trinitarian model. Defenders of a trinitarian paradigm troubled other fathers, however, with their decision to employ new terms not found in the Bible — among them *homoousios* — to picture and elucidate the implications of the biblical data and the church's practice, particularly in worship.

The conclusions reached at Nicea (325 CE) were debated and not infrequently rejected for a period of more than fifty years. Some fathers rejected Nicea because, as we have mentioned, they felt its newly coined terms — again *homoousios* comes to mind — went too far beyond the boundaries of the biblical testimony itself. These theologians, sympathetic to Nicea and theologically conservative, longed to see creedal statements more firmly tied to the Bible. The supporters of Arius continued to argue that the testimony of Scripture surely gave an exalted position to Christ, but did not teach that he was divine and uncreated.

Perhaps the best path we can follow is to trace the church's steps back to the beginning of the second century and then travel forward with Christian bishops, pastors, exegetes, and theologians. Indeed, patristic theology is in many ways exegesis, the struggle — sometimes more, sometimes less successful — of early Christian interpreters to make sense out of the biblical testimony concerning Father, Son, and Holy Spirit.

Early Ante-Nicene Contributions[1]

What do we find in the writings of Christian leaders during roughly the first sixty years of the second century CE? As we might expect, we do not find the developed trinitarian language or theology that will blossom from the fourth century on. We do, however, uncover evidence that early second-century writers were already noticing, analyzing, and struggling with the implications of the Hebrew scriptures, apostolic testimony, and the church's worship in their attempt to understand God's nature and work.

The bishop Clement, writing in the last years of the first century CE, repeatedly refers to the Father, Son, and the Holy Spirit. He particularly

---

1. For all quotations from the apostolic fathers, cf. *The Apostolic Fathers*, second edition, trans. J. B. Lightfoot and J. R. Harmer, edited and revised by Michael W. Holmes (Grand Rapids: Baker Book House, 1989).

links the Father to creation: ". . . let us fix our eyes upon the Father and Maker of the whole world" (1 Clement 19:2). The "gifts of God," including "immortality, splendor in righteousness, and truth with boldness," find their source in the "Creator and Father of the ages," who "knows their number and their beauty" (1 Clement 35:1-3). It is through "his beloved servant Jesus Christ" that "the Creator of the universe" keeps the elect of God "intact" (1 Clement 59:2). Clement describes Jesus as the Creator's "servant," the "majestic scepter of God, our Lord Christ Jesus" (1 Clement 16:2).

The Holy Spirit frequently appears in 1 Clement. It is the Spirit, Clement writes, who has inspired the Scripture (1 Clement 45:2), and Christ himself speaks through the Holy Spirit (1 Clement 22:1). In a striking phrase Clement joins together the Father, Son, and Holy Spirit, encouraging his reader to remember that just as these three live, so those who humbly and gently obey God's commandments can be sure they are "enrolled and included" among the number of the elect. Clement also groups Father, Son, and Spirit in the context of apostolic mission (1 Clement 42:1-4) and calling. For example, Clement asks, "Do we not have one God and one Christ and one Spirit of grace which was poured out upon us? And is there not one calling in Christ?" (1 Clement 46:6). It is texts such as these that Basil the Great will later recall and develop in his own trinitarian reflection.[2] In the late first century, then, we have a Christian bishop sprinkling nuggets of trinitarian ore throughout his writing that will later be mined and purified.

We have the same kind of sprinkling effect in the letters of Ignatius, bishop of Antioch. Ignatius penned these letters as he was led under Roman guard to execution in Rome. In them Ignatius employs elevated language as he speaks of the Father, Son, and Holy Spirit. For instance, in his introduction to his letter to the church in Ephesus, Ignatius writes of the Ephesians as "united and elect through genuine suffering by the will of the Father and of Jesus Christ our God" (intro.). Later in the same letter Ignatius describes Christ "as the mind of the Father" (Ephesians 1:30), "our Savior" (Ephesians 1:1), and "our inseparable life" (Ephesians 1:3). The christological and at least binitarian implications of Ignatius' description of the incarnation are also quite remarkable as seen in his reference to

---

2. Cf. Edward J. Fortman, *The Triune God: A Historical Study of the Doctrine of the Trinity* (Philadelphia: Westminster, 1972), p. 38.

Christ as "both flesh and spirit, born and unborn, god in man, true life in death, both from Mary and from God . . ." (Ephesians 7:2). Ignatius insists that Jesus was born from both human seed and "of the Holy Spirit" (Ephesians 1:18). In perhaps his most striking statement regarding the Father, Son, and Holy Spirit Ignatius writes that the Ephesian church is "the building of God the Father, hoisted up to the heights by the crane of Jesus Christ, which is the cross, using as a rope the Holy Spirit . . ." (Ephesians 9:1).

Ignatius, like Clement before him, is not writing as a theologian to defend the creeds of the church. Rather, he is a bishop writing to encourage, exhort, and comfort his flock as he sees his life drawing to a close. All the more significant, then, are the trinitarian implications of his language, seeds that will later sprout in the thought of an Athanasius or Basil.

Other early second-century documents illustrate well the difficulty ancient Christian writers faced in struggling to make sense of the unity and plurality of God. *The Shepherd of Hermas,* an extremely popular writing that was accorded canonical status by figures such as Irenaeus, Clement of Alexandria, and Origen, rightly insisted that there is only one God. Hermas, though, struggled to make sense of the Son and Spirit. Indeed, Hermas appears to fall into a number of errors also repeated by later theologians. For example, it is not clear whether Hermas considered the Son to be an angel or more ancient than the angels. Occasionally he blurs the distinction between the Son and the Spirit, and in one instance seemingly unites them, writing that "the Spirit is the Son of God" (Parable 9.1.78). In other places Hermas demonstrates adoptionist tendencies, as in his parable of the vineyard (Parable 5). Although we find support for the unity of God in Hermas' writing, his struggle to define the plurality of God was characteristic of his time.

Glimpses of early church order and practice and its understanding of God can be found in catechetical documents such as *The Didache.* God is addressed as "Father" in prayer (*Didache* 8:2; 10:2), and is also called "Father" in a trinitarian baptismal formula ("baptize 'in the name of the Father and of the Son and of the Holy Spirit,'" *Didache* 7:3). Jesus is most often referred to as "Lord": ". . . just as the Lord commanded" (*Didache* 8:2). *The Didache* also mentions baptism as taking place "into the name of the Lord" (*Didache* 9:5). The Aramaic word *maranatha* occurs once ("our Lord, come") in *Didache* 10:6. Any mention of the Holy Spirit is limited to the baptismal formulas in *Didache* 7:1 and 7:3. Though brief catechetical documents such as *The Didache* contain no explicit trinitarian reflection, they remain important because they provide the nutrients for the soil of the church's trinitarian seedbed.

We can find other hints of the complex nature of God in early accounts of Christian martyrdom, such as that of the bishop Polycarp. The martyrdom of Polycarp, perhaps the oldest martyrdom of which we have a written account (ca. early 160s CE), pictures the dying Polycarp addressing God in a clear triadic confession: "O Lord God Almighty, Father of your beloved Son Jesus Christ . . . I bless you because you have considered me worthy of this day and hour, that I might receive a place among the number of the martyrs . . . to the resurrection to eternal life . . . in the incorruptibility of the Holy Spirit" (*The Martyrdom of Polycarp* 14:1-2).

Later in the account of Polycarp's martyrdom we find a careful distinction made between Christ and Christ's martyrs. Christ "who is the Son of God, we worship, but the martyrs we love as disciples and imitators of the Lord" (*The Martyrdom of Polycarp* 17:3). Elevated prayers and doxologies such as those found in the account of Polycarp's death will soon lead to necessary theological developments. Hence, not only the Scripture, but also the worship and prayer of the church will prove to be the bedrock and garden of its theology. Athanasius will later argue, for example, that if Christians have worshiped and continue to worship Christ, he must be considered God. To admit otherwise would be to accuse the church of continuous blasphemy in its prayer and practice, from the first century onwards.

Two final early second-century documents also help us to understand why the unity and plurality of God would inevitably become a topic of theological reflection, discussion, and controversy. In *The Epistle of Barnabas* we find an early Christian writer sifting through the pages of the Hebrew scriptures for texts illustrating the fulfillment of God's purposes in Christ. Barnabas presents Christ as pre-existent, describing him as the one "to whom God said at the foundation of the world, 'Let us make man according to our image and likeness'" (*The Epistle of Barnabas* 5:5). In the same text Barnabas pictures the Son as "the Lord of the whole world." This epistle sometimes calls God the "Father" (cf. *The Epistle of Barnabas* 2:9; 12:8). Less is said about the Holy Spirit, though the epistle does speak of the Spirit instructing Moses "to make a symbol of the cross" (*The Epistle of Barnabas* 12:2).

We close our survey of early post-apostolic documents with the mention of *2 Clement,* a document that perhaps first appeared in sermon form around 100 CE. The opening line of the sermon immediately catches the eye: "Brothers, we ought to think of Jesus Christ, as we do of God, as 'Judge of the living and the dead'" (*2 Clement* 1:1). Note should also be taken of the closing doxology: "'To the only God, invisible,' the Father of truth, who sent forth to us the truth and the heavenly life, to him be glory forever and ever. Amen" (*2 Clement* 20:5).

Of course, the question later Christians will struggle to answer is: How can we think of Jesus Christ as God while simultaneously maintaining that the Father is "the only God"? In *2 Clement,* the writer quite clearly is struggling with the same kind of question, sometimes less successfully than his Christian descendants. He seems, for example, to blur the distinction between Christ and the Spirit in his moral exhortations to his listeners: "Now if we say that the flesh is the church and the Spirit is Christ, then the one who abuses the flesh abuses the church. Consequently such a person will not receive the Spirit, which is Christ" (*2 Clement* 14:4). Again, we sense an early Christian writer attempting to understand coherently the complex biblical, liturgical, and devotional testimony he had received concerning Father, Son, and Spirit. High marks on the relationship between Father and Son. Less so on the Son and Spirit.

We will be disappointed if we expect to find developed trinitarian reflection in the early post-apostolic writers. It is simply not there. More time will be needed for the implications of early Christian thought and practice to ferment and mature. Thus, church historians and theologians often begin their treatment of the doctrine of the Trinity with the second-century apologists.[3] We would err, though, if we passed over the post-apostolic period too quickly. For it is during these early years of the church's life, roughly 100-150 CE, that many trinitarian questions, issues, and problems begin to bubble to the surface of the church's thinking. It is, for example, becoming increasingly clear to the early Christian community that the picture of God presented in the narrative of the gospel is both complex and mysterious. Post-apostolic writers insist on the unity of God, while simultaneously acknowledging that it is fitting for the church to worship Christ as God. How Christ can be God and Christians still maintain the unity of God will be a question increasingly discussed in the years

3. Cf. Gerald O'Collins, S.J., *The Tripersonal God: Understanding and Interpreting the Trinity* (New York: Paulist Press, 1999), pp. 85-103.

to come. As we have seen, post-apostolic writers also pondered the relationship between Christ and the Spirit, sometimes considering the two to be identical. It is in the work of early Christian apologists such as Justin Martyr that these issues will assume greater clarity and form.

The Apologists

As we move into the second half of the second century CE, we meet an early Ante-Nicene apologist for the Christian faith: Justin Martyr (110-165 CE). Justin Martyr exerted much effort in responding to Jewish objections to the possibility that Jesus of Nazareth could be the promised Messiah. In Justin's *Dialogue with Trypho* he deals directly with the question of Christ's divinity, its implications for Christ's relationship with the Father, and the relationship of Christ's divine nature to his life as a genuine human being. Similar arguments and analysis appear in Justin's *First Apology*.

Justin consistently argues that the Hebrew scriptures point to the divinity of Israel's long awaited Messiah. In response to Trypho's request for proof "that He submitted to become man by the Virgin, according to the will of His Father; and to be crucified, and to die" (chapter 63), Justin lists a long chain of Old Testament texts. Justin seems to believe that these texts self-evidently point to the incarnation and comments: "Therefore these words testify explicitly that He is witnessed to by Him who established these things, as deserving to be worshipped, as God and as Christ" (chapter 63).

Justin realizes, though, that if he asserts the divinity of Jesus another set of questions will immediately present themselves: If Jesus is God, how can Christians claim to worship only one God?[4] Is Jesus God in the same manner as the Father? Or is he perhaps a lesser divinity? If Christ, the Father, and the Spirit are all God, in what way are they distinct? Is the Son distinct from the Spirit? If Father, Son, and Spirit share the same mind, does this mean that they share the same consciousness?[5]

How can one best describe the relationship between the Father and the Son? Justin refers to Christ in a variety of ways, including "Lord," "God the Son of God," and "the Word." As the "Word," Jesus "carries tidings

4. We have found Gerald O'Collins's discussion of Justin to be quite helpful. Cf. O'Collins, *The Tripersonal God*, pp. 87-96.

5. Cf. O'Collins, *The Tripersonal God*, p. 90.

from the Father to men." The power the Word exerts, however, is "indivisible and inseparable from the Father." How so? Here Justin employs an illustration destined to appear again and again in the trinitarian thought of the fathers. Think, Justin asks his audience, of the sunlight that reaches the earth. While this light is distinct from the sun in the heavens, it is equally "indivisible and inseparable" from it. It is much the same with a fire igniting another fire. So it is with the begetting of the Son. The unbegotten Father begets the Son, "but not by amputation, as if the essence of the Father were divided."[6] Here, as Gerald O'Collins notes, Justin "anticipated a question that was to be long debated in the fourth century, the consubstantiality (or being of 'one essence') of the Father and the Son (or Word) in that they share the same essence or *ousia*."[7]

Not only does Justin anticipate future discussions of the consubstantiality of the Father and Son, but he is the first to connect Christ with the Wisdom of God mentioned in Proverbs 8:22. He inaugurates a lasting patristic image — "light from light" — that is later incorporated in the Nicene Creed and initiates the patristic understanding of Genesis 1:26 as referring at least to the Father and the Son joining together in the creation of humanity.[8] Justin's tendency to speak of the Son as an "Angel" received a much cooler reception among later fathers. He was also less successful in his willingness to refer to the Son as "another God besides the Creator," language that could easily lead to a subordinationist model of intra-trinitarian relations.[9]

Indeed, as Russell Norris, Jr., points out, Justin's willingness to employ a *logos* model to *explain* the meaning of Christ as the "Son of God," rather than simply associating the two terms, does lead to problems.[10] Justin argues that the "begetting" of the Son is similar to the manner in which a "rational mind *(logos)* expresses itself in a rational word *(logos)*. The *logos*, as God's 'Word,' is in a sense God's 'Son,' and the 'begetting' of the *logos* is accomplished when God 'speaks' him and 'sends him forth.'"[11] Norris observes, the problem is that the movement from God's Word thought to God's Word spoken, i.e., as

6. Justin Martyr, *Dialogue*, 128; quoted in O'Collins, *The Tripersonal God*, p. 89.

7. O'Collins, *The Tripersonal God*, p. 89.

8. O'Collins, *The Tripersonal God*, p. 89.

9. O'Collins, *The Tripersonal God*, p. 90.

10. Russell Bradner Norris, Jr., "Logos Christology as Cosmological Paradigm," *Pro Ecclesia* 5, no. 2, p. 191.

11. Norris, "Logos Christology," p. 191.

becoming the "Son of God," suggests change within the *logos,* a problem Norris observes to be true of Theophilus of Antioch's distinction between the *logos endiathetos* and the *logos prophorikos.*

Still, even if Justin occasionally swerves off the path, his willingness to listen to the church at worship, in its prayers, liturgies, and creedal confessions, generally kept him moving in the right direction. In his *First Apology* he writes: "We revere and worship him [the true God], and the Son, who came from him and taught us these things . . . and the prophetic Spirit."[12] Justin seemed to realize that if the church worshiped Father, Son, and Spirit, a trinitarian model of some kind must be forthcoming, and he provided important planks in its construction.

Early Alexandrian Contributions

Clement of Alexandria sprinkles scattered references or allusions to trinitarian considerations in both *The Instructor (Paidagogos)* and in the *Stromata.* Near the beginning of *The Instructor,* for example, Clement offers a "Prayer to the Paedagogus," an early Christian petition and doxology to the Father, Son, and Holy Spirit.[13] Also of interest is Clement's rich allusion to the protection offered by "the power of God the Father, and the blood of God the Son, and the dew of the Holy Spirit," in his sermon "Who Is the Rich Man That Shall Be Saved?"[14]

Readers might turn to Book 7, chapter 2 of the *Stromata* for a hermeneutical sampling of Clement's reflections on the relationship between the Father and Son. Clement describes the Son as "the most perfect, and most holy, and most potent, and most princely, and most kingly, and most beneficent." It is the Son "who orders all things in accordance with the Father's will, and holds the helm of the universe in the best way, with unwearied and tireless power. . . ." The Son "is never displaced; not being divided, not severed, not passing from place to place; being always everywhere, and being contained nowhere, complete mind, the complete paternal light."[15]

12. Justin Martyr, *First Apology,* 6; quoted in O'Collins, *The Tripersonal God,* p. 95.

13. Clement of Alexandria, *The Instructor,* ANF, vol. 2 (Peabody, Mass.: Hendrickson, 1994), p. 295.

14. Clement of Alexandria, "Who Is the Rich Man That Shall Be Saved?", ANF, vol. 2 (Peabody, Mass.: Hendrickson, 1994), para. 34, p. 601.

15. Clement of Alexandria, *Stromata,* ANF, vol. 2, book 7, p. 524. For a recent transla-

In *On First Principles (De Principiis)*, Origen, the great Alexandrian exegete, provides important and interesting examples of a theologian's attempts to understand the biblical testimony and rule of faith concerning Father, Son, and Holy Spirit. Origen sometimes strays in his musings and constructions, but his contributions to trinitarian thinking cannot be ignored.[16]

Origen understands that the generation of the Son cannot possibly be a corporeal generation. "For we do not say, as the heretics suppose, that some part of the substance of God was converted into the Son, or that the Son was procreated by the Father out of things non-existent, i.e., beyond His own substance, so that there was a time when He did not exist." No, Origen insists, corporeal constructions will lead nowhere. Rather, the Son "was begotten out of the invisible and incorporeal without any corporeal feeling, as if it were an act of the will proceeding from the understanding. . . ." Origen turns to the familiar patristic illustration of light and its source to make his point. "As light, accordingly, could never exist without splendor, so neither can the Son be understood to exist without the Father."

In a preview of coming debates, Origen wonders how anyone could assert "that there once was a time when He was not the Son." Has the Father ever existed without his "express image"? To assert that there was ever a time when the Son did not exist would be to contend "there was once a time when He was not the Truth, nor the Wisdom, nor the Life, although in all these He is judged to be the perfect essence of God the Father, for these things cannot be severed from Him, or even be separated from His essence. . . ."[17]

And yet Origen is not always successful or consistent in his attempt to make sense of the nature of the Son and his relationship to the Father. On the one hand, Origen writes that "if our Savior knows all that is known by the Father . . . it must be understood that he is the Savior because he is the

---

tion of the first three books of the *Stromata*, cf. Clement of Alexandria, *Stromateis*, Fathers of the Church, vol. 85, trans. John Ferguson (Washington, D.C.: Catholic University of America Press, 1991).

16. Cf. Origen, *On First Principles*, ANF, vol. 4 (Peabody, Mass.: Hendrickson, 1994). Readers should particularly consult Origen's preface, section 4; book 1, chapters 1-3 (chapter 1 "on God," chapter 2 "on Christ," and chapter 3 "on the Holy Spirit"; book 2, chapter 4 (on the identity of the God of the Old Testament and the Father of Jesus Christ), chapter 6 (on the incarnation of Christ), and chapter 7 (on the Holy Spirit). Cf. also Origen's summary in book 4, "regarding the Father, Son, and Holy Spirit," ANF, vol. 4, pp. 376-82.

17. Origen, *On First Principles*, ANF, vol. 4, book 4, chapter 28, pp. 376-77.

Truth, and further that if he is the whole Truth, he knows everything that is true."[18] On the other hand, Origen also asserts that "in respect of knowledge the Father is known by himself more fully and clearly and completely than he is known by the Son."[19] Origen occasionally argues that there are degrees of divinity, and sometimes views matters proportionally: the Father : the Son (and the Holy Spirit) : all created beings.[20] "We say that the Son and the Holy Spirit excel all created beings to a degree which admits of no comparison, and are themselves excelled by the Father to the same or even greater degree."[21] Origen fails to explain adequately how there can be this kind of proportionality within the shared divine nature of Father, Son, and Spirit, appearing to be trapped by his Platonic background. If the Father was the cause of the Son, even by an eternal generation, "a consistent Platonism must conclude," as Cary notes, "that he is subordinate in being, lower in dignity, and less in power."[22]

Origen's thinking on the Holy Spirit is also a mixed bag. He recognizes that the Spirit "is a substantial being. It is not, as some imagine, an activity of God without individual existence." For the Spirit both "wills" and "distributes" spiritual gifts, the activity of an "active substance."[23] Origen clearly states that "Up to the present I have been able to find no passage in the Scriptures that the Holy Spirit is a created being. . . ."[24] And still, as we have seen, Origen can write that the Spirit is excelled by the Father to the same degree that the Spirit excelled "all created beings."

Origen serves as an apt model, perhaps because of his creative, innovative mind, of the struggle of the fathers to say enough about the Trinity, but not too much. At times he seems to violate his own advice. He rightly counsels his audience, for example, to avoid imagining the "begetting" of the Son as "equivalent to the begetting of man by man or animal by animal; there must needs be a great difference . . . since nothing can be found in existence, or conceived or imagined, to compare with God." For, Origen

18. Origen, *Comm. In Joannem*, 1.27; quoted in *The Early Christian Fathers*, ed. and trans. Henry Bettenson (Oxford University Press, 1956), p. 322.

19. Origen, *De Principiis*, 4.35; quoted in *The Early Christian Fathers*, p. 322.

20. *The Early Christian Fathers*, p. 322.

21. Origen, *Comm. In Joannem* 13.25; quoted in *The Early Christian Fathers*, p. 322.

22. Phillip Cary, "Historical Perspectives on Trinitarian Doctrine," *Religious and Theological Studies Fellowship Bulletin* (November-December 1995): 2-3.

23. Origen, *In Ioannem Fragmenta*, 37; quoted in *The Early Christian Fathers*, p. 313.

24. Origen, *De Principiis*, 1.3.3; quoted in *The Early Christian Fathers*, p. 315.

observes, "human thought cannot apprehend how the unbegotten God becomes the Father of the only-begotten Son," a generation Origen describes as "eternal" and "ceaseless." Origen, though, exceeds his own advice, proposing models rooted in his Platonic background that will later be rejected as failing to preserve the mystery of the Trinity by trying to explain too much. In the effort to help us understand, Origen ends up leading us away from the ineffable truth of the matter.[25]

Early Western Contributions

Modern readers would do well to consult the work of Irenaeus closely, especially as his theological reflection is a specific response to the widespread gnosticism of his day, not entirely unlike the blossoming of gnosticism in the late twentieth century. Among other things, Irenaeus believed his gnostic opponents claimed to know too much. They had produced complex, well-nigh indecipherable works purportedly plumbing the metaphysics and mechanics of creation itself, the relation between matter (by definition evil), spirit (by definition good), and salvation (viewed as the ascent from the material world to the realm of pure spirit). As Irenaeus criticizes gnostic cosmology, he is careful to describe his own theological methodology. In response to the gnostics' inflated claims to knowledge of divine mysteries, Irenaeus advocates a much more restrained, sober course. He speaks of a "proper order of . . . knowledge" and warns his readers not to "seek to rise above God himself." No one can fully understand the nature and purposes of God. To forget this will only lead to "trains of reflection opposed to your nature," with the final outcome a predictable foolishness.[26]

Irenaeus' phrase, "preserve . . . the proper order of your knowledge," captures well a continuing emphasis in patristic trinitarian thinking. The church fathers never believed, either in the Ante-Nicene or Post-Nicene

25. Readers might find Origen's response to Celsus to be of interest. Celsus, a fervent critic of Christianity, was convinced that Christians not only worshiped God but creatures, "servants" of God. Origen fumbles somewhat in his response, writing that the Son is "inferior" to the Father, while simultaneously writing that the Father and Son, "two persons," are both worshiped by the Christian community. Cf. Origen, *Against Celsus,* ANF, vol. 4, book 8, chapters 12-15.

26. Irenaeus, *Against Heresies,* ANF, vol. 1 (Peabody, Mass.: Hendrickson, 1994), book 2.25.3-4, p. 397.

periods, that they could rationally explicate the mystery of God's triune nature. Almost inevitably, it seems, heresy erupts in the patristic period when people try to say too much, rather than too little. Thus, church fathers such as Irenaeus were more interested in theological boundaries than theological expansiveness. Yes, they would say, we have discovered that God is more complex than we would have ever imagined left to ourselves. Yes, we can affirm that Father, Son, and Holy Spirit share the same divine nature, are one God, and yet distinct within that ineffable unity. But the reality we are attempting to comprehend, study, describe, and worship cannot be contained or fully grasped within "the order" of our knowledge. In short, whether it be an Irenaeus rebuking gnostic teachers in the second century, or a Gregory of Nazianzus chastising Eunomian mavericks in the fourth century, both would contend and affirm that theological understanding is necessarily limited. It must be pursued within certain boundaries and orders, and nurtured within the context of worship and devotion.

Irenaeus, of course, is interested in more than theological methodology and epistemology. His foremost work, *Against Heresies,* is filled with christological and trinitarian insights engendered and shaped in his opposition to the ideas of both Marcion and the second-century gnostics. Marcion, for instance, had taught that the God of the Old Testament, a God Marcion pictured as angry and vindictive, could not possibly be the God revealed in Jesus Christ. Irenaeus rebuked Marcion for dividing "God into two," calling "one God good and the other just. In so doing he destroys the divinity of both."[27] Irenaeus here plays a key role in helping the church to understand two key points, both to be reinforced in the Nicene-Constantinopolitan Creed: first, there is only one God. As Gerald O'Collins phrases it: "There cannot be more than one case of deity." Second, we can't throw up a hedge between the God of the old covenant and the God revealed in Jesus Christ. The two are actually one and the same. "The Jewish Creator God is identical with the *Father* of our Lord Jesus Christ."[28]

Irenaeus also lays important groundwork in his explanation of the eternal generation of the Son by the Father. He admits he does not understand how the Son is "produced" from the Father, and sharply critiques the

---

27. Irenaeus, *Against Heresies,* book 3.25.3; quoted in O'Collins, *The Tripersonal God,* p. 97.

28. O'Collins, *The Tripersonal God,* p. 97.

gnostics for claiming to know too much on a topic that is genuinely inde-scribable. Irenaeus affirms the eternality of the Son as an attribute of deity and offers fairly muted illustrations of how this generation might take place.[29] He employs what will later be known as the "psychological" model, picturing the generation of the Son like "a thought emerging from our mind or a word from our lips," an illustration also to be used by Athanasius.[30] Irenaeus also employs a less successful model of the Father "emitting" the Logos like a "material substance." This illustration seems to necessitate a beginning in time. Nicea's specific confession of the Son as "begotten, not made," rejects specifically the possibility of a temporal gen-eration.[31]

Irenaeus, like almost all church fathers, was deeply concerned to pro-tect the transcendence of the Father, while equally insisting that God has entered his world in the incarnation of the Son. Thus, Irenaeus employs his famous description of the Son and Spirit as the "two hands" of God in "carrying out his intended work of creation." Contra gnostic speculations, God "did not need any help from angels, as if he did not have his own hands. For he always had at his side his Word and Wisdom, the Son and the Spirit."[32]

Interestingly, while many fathers identify the personified Wisdom of Proverbs 8 with the Son, Irenaeus identifies it with the Spirit.[33] "We have shown at length that the Word, that is the Son, was always with the Father. And God tells us, through the mouth of Solomon, that Wisdom, that is the Spirit, was with him before the whole creation. . . ."[34] In addition, Irenaeus describes the key role of the Spirit in a "kind of vertical, trinitarian line starting from the Spirit to the Son, and continuing upward from the Son to the Father."[35] "The Spirit," Irenaeus writes, "prepares human beings for the

29. Cf. O'Collins, *The Tripersonal God*, pp. 98-99.

30. O'Collins, *The Tripersonal God*, p. 99. O'Collins explains that here we again have the idea of the *logos endiathetos* ("the immanent word 'emitted' from the mind"), and the "exterior word in human speech *(logos prophorikos)*."

31. Cf. O'Collins, *The Tripersonal God*, p. 99.

32. Irenaeus, *Against Heresies*, book 4.20.1; quoted in O'Collins, *The Tripersonal God*, p. 99.

33. For Irenaeus on the Spirit, cf. *Against Heresies*, ANF, vol. 1, 1.10.1, 3.17.2, 3.18.3, 3.24.1, 3.9.2-3, 4.20.3-4, 5.1.2, 5.12.2, 5.13.4, 5.18.2, 5.36.2, 5.8.1, 5.9.1.

34. Irenaeus, *Against Heresies*, book 4.20.3; quoted in O'Collins, *The Tripersonal God*, p. 101.

35. O'Collins, *The Tripersonal God*, p. 101.

Son of God; the Son leads them to the Father; the Father gives them immortality. . . . Thus God was revealed: for in all these ways God the Father is displayed. The Spirit works, the Son fulfills his ministry, the Father approves."[36]

In Tertullian we encounter one of the finest theological minds to appear in the Latin West. Tertullian's *Against Praxeas* remains indispensable reading for students of trinitarian doctrine and its development. In this work we find Tertullian pondering central trinitarian issues and responding to heterodox Christian views regarding the Father, Son, and Holy Spirit. In his responses and formulations, Tertullian coined a Latin trinitarian vocabulary that remained highly influential. He was, for example, the first writer to use the word "person" in an analysis of trinitarian relationships, the first to apply the Latin word *trinitas* to God, and the first "to develop the formula of *one substance in three persons*."[37]

Tertullian, like Christian theologians both before and after him, faced a number of challenges. How was he to defend Christian monotheism against the gnostic polytheists, while simultaneously maintaining the personal distinctions between the Father, Son, and Spirit, distinctions that forms of Christian modalism threatened?

In *Against Praxeas,* Tertullian's main antagonist staunchly defended the "one principle" or *mone arche* of God's being. That is to say, any distinctions within the being of God and manifested in the economy of salvation must be modes through which the one principle of God, the Father, was manifesting itself. To posit otherwise, Praxeas contended, would necessarily destroy a coherent monotheism. Hence, only the Father existed ontologically. It was the Father, then, who actually died on the cross (patripassianism). Slightly later in the third century Sabellius was to de-

36. Irenaeus, *Against Heresies,* book 4.20.4, 6; quoted in O'Collins, *The Tripersonal God,* p. 102. Because of the length and tangled nature of *Against Heresies,* the following christological and trinitarian road map may prove helpful: book 2.28.6, 2.30.9, 3.6.1, 3.9.3, 3.10.2, 4.1-2, 4.5-7, 4.20, 5.17-18, 5.21. In book 3.19, for instance, Irenaeus writes that "Jesus Christ was not a mere man . . . but was very God." Irenaeus' christology from *Against Heresies* can be supplemented by *Fragments from the Lost Writings of Irenaeus,* 52-54, ANF, vol. 1, pp. 576-77. These fragments are largely christological in nature, clearly representing Irenaeus' consistent contention that the Father and Son are one God, not two, and surely not part of a chain of aeons or angels — a common gnostic contention.

37. O'Collins, *The Tripersonal God,* p. 105. We have found O'Collins's summary of Tertullian's thought on the Trinity to be quite helpful.

fend a similar but modified position, dividing salvation history into three distinct periods in which God manifested the divine presence: the Father during the Old Covenant, the Son during the incarnation and redemption, and the Spirit at Pentecost.[38]

Tertullian constructed his model of God as one substance *(substantia)* and three distinct persons *(persona)* in response to the threat of both gnostic polytheism and Christian modalism. He taught that God is one *substantia,* a term helpfully defined by Gerald O'Collins as "the common fundamental reality shared by Father, Son, and Holy Spirit."[39] Tertullian knew, though, that more needed to be said. God's *substantia* was marked by a mysterious, ineffable complexity that could only be analyzed by means of analogy. Three distinct persons shared the one substance of God, a personhood identified by the names Father, Son, and Holy Spirit. Unfortunately, *hypostasis* was often the Greek translation of *substantia,* creating significant confusion as the Greeks applied *hypostasis* to the persons rather than the divine substance.

What analogies might illustrate well these mysterious distinctions? Tertullian uses one we have already encountered with other fathers, that of the sun and its light. He expands it a bit, though. The sun (the Father) "produces" a ray (the Son) that then has a particular focus (the Spirit). Tertullian also adds the example of a root producing a shoot, which in turn produces fruit, and that of a spring feeding a river which feeds a canal. He emphasizes that "none of these is divorced from the origin from which it derives its own properties. Thus the Trinity derives from the Father by continuous and connected steps."[40] The distinctions, therefore, within the Trinity are not substantial (resulting in polytheism or tritheism), but personal.

One needs to be careful at this point, however, for we are apt to apply anachronistically a current understanding of "person" to Tertullian's model, one that might lead us to think of Father, Son, and Spirit as possessing a separate self-consciousness or as existing as autonomous individuals. Personal distinctions within the Trinity do not mean separateness or autonomy. In fact, Tertullian describes the Son or second person of the Trinity as the Reason or *Ratio* of the Father, first existing in the mind of the

38. O'Collins, *The Tripersonal God,* p. 104.
39. O'Collins, *The Tripersonal God,* p. 105.
40. Tertullian, *Against Praxeas,* 8; quoted in O'Collins, *The Tripersonal God,* p. 106.

Father and then expressed as his *sermo* or "speech."[41] We have here simultaneous distinction and unity, rather than autonomy and separation.

At times Tertullian stumbles in his attempt to explain trinitarian relationships. For instance, he describes the Father as "the whole substance [of deity], while the Son is derivative and a portion of the whole. . . ."[42] Unguarded statements such as these could easily lead to the impression that the Son is somewhat lesser in his deity than the Father. It is also difficult to see how the divine *substantia* could be divided or portioned out, like servings of mashed potatoes. Despite occasional missteps, though, Tertullian proves to be a reliable guide, ably avoiding the twin hazards of tritheism and modalism.[43]

Key Eastern Figures from the Age of Nicea and Beyond

We can glean the views of Arius, the central theological antagonist of "orthodoxy" in the fourth century CE, only from the writings of his opponents. Athanasius, the bishop of Alexandria, proves to be our main source for the thought and positions of Arius. Is Athanasius always representing

41. Tertullian, *Against Praxeas,* 5; quoted in O'Collins, *The Tripersonal God,* p. 107.

42. Tertullian, *Against Praxeas,* 9; quoted in O'Collins, *The Tripersonal God,* p. 107.

43. O'Collins observes that Tertullian, like many other fathers, identified the Word with the personalized Wisdom of Proverbs 8. O'Collins comments: "Tertullian's identification of the Word/Son as divine Wisdom fitted into a broad consensus among the patristic authors, but any literal version of God truly '*creating* his Word' had no future in mainline trinitarian teaching, which would be built around Nicaea's eternally 'begotten' but not at some point willingly 'made/created'" (*The Tripersonal God,* p. 108). A helpful summary of Tertullian's understanding of the church's rule of faith on Father, Son, and Spirit can be found in *Against Praxeas,* ANF, vol. 3 (Peabody, Mass.: Hendrickson, 1994), chapter 2, p. 598. Cf. also Tertullian's *Apology,* ANF, vol. 3. Chapter 21 of the *Apology* contains a nice example of Tertullian's illustrations of trinitarian relationships: "Even when the ray is shot from the sun, it is still part of the parent mass; the sun will still be in the ray, because it is a ray of the sun — there is no division of substance, but merely an extension. Thus Christ is Spirit of Spirit, and God of God, as light of light is kindled" (p. 34). The metaphor of sun and light will continue to be a favorite patristic illustration of the relationship between the Father and Son (cf. Tertullian, *Against Marcion,* ANF, vol. 3, book 2, chapter 27). Readers interested in Tertullian's understanding and explanation of the unity of God should consult *Against Marcion,* book 1, chapters 3-7, pp. 273-76. As for christological issues, cf. Tertullian, *On the Flesh of Christ,* ANF, vol. 3, chapter 18. In this text, for example, Tertullian addresses the question of whether Jesus possessed a genuine human body.

Arius fairly? Probably not. Still, we are forced to rely largely on Athanasius' quotations from Arius' *Thalia*.

Although we cannot be absolutely sure of Arius' exact words, we can be confident that Arius struggled mightily with the possibility that the Son could share the Father's divinity. The subordinationist tendencies that had plagued Origen deeply manifested themselves in Arius. Arius seems to have viewed the generation of the Son as a process, a danger of the *logos endia-thetos/logos prophorikos* model when in Platonic hands. In addition, he "objected to the idea that in coming forth from the Father the Son took some of that substance with him, thus dividing the Father's substance and lessening him."[44] The Word could not belong to the Father's substance. Instead, Arius argued that the Son was an exalted creature, elevated above all others, but still a creation of God. Arius writes, for instance, that "God was not always a Father," "The Son was not always," "the Word of God Himself was 'made out of nothing,'" "once He was not," "He was not before His origination," and "He as others 'had an origin of creation.'"[45] "For God," Arius taught, "was alone, and the Word as yet was not, nor the Wisdom. Then, wishing to form us, thereupon He made a certain one, and named him Word and Wisdom and Son, that he might form us by means of Him."[46]

Arius' insistence that the Son was a created being spawned the rich christological theology of the fourth century and, towards its conclusion, the much-needed exploration of the person and work of the Holy Spirit.[47] Athanasius' own exegesis and theology is inseparably linked to his lifelong battle with Arianism. His *Four Discourses Against the Arians* provide us with many examples of how Athanasius read the Bible and applied its contents to a specific theological problem of great moment.

As we have seen, Arian Christians refused to equate the Son with the Father, basing this rejection on philosophical, theological, and exegetical reasons. To focus only on the biblical question, Arian exegetes observed that many New Testament texts spoke quite openly and clearly of Jesus' humanity. In the garden of Gethsemane Jesus experienced grief and fear. Would a divine being experience and express these emotions and responses? What

44. Cary, "Historical Perspectives on Trinitarian Doctrine," p. 3.

45. Athanasius, *Four Discourses Against the Arians*, NPNF Second Series, vol. 4 (Peabody, Mass.: Hendrickson, 1994), pp. 308-9.

46. Athanasius, *Four Discourses Against the Arians*, pp. 308-9.

47. For further direct quotations by Athanasius from Arius's *Thalia*, cf. Athanasius, *Four Discourses Against the Arians*, Discourse 1, chapter 2.

of the questions Jesus asked during his lifetime? For example, Jesus seems to have acknowledged his own ignorance as to the time when all things would "be accomplished" (cf. Mark 13:4, 32). Thus, the Father's knowledge appears clearly to be greater than that of the Son. If so, how could Father and Son share the same divinity? Shared divinity necessitated shared attributes. If the Son was ignorant of key matters such as the timing of the consummation of the age, he by definition could not be divine.

Athanasius' exegetical and theological response to the Arian position, developed in *Four Discourses Against the Arians* and the background music to many of his works, in part analyzed the relationship between Christ's deity and humanity. Athanasius contended that the "scope and character" of Scripture contained a "double account of the Savior." The Bible, Athanasius insisted, affirmed *both* the deity and humanity of Christ. The Arians' exegesis failed to recognize that some biblical texts referred specifically to issues, events, or teachings related to Christ's humanity, while others related to his actions as *God* incarnate.

As the Son, Christ existed as "the Father's Word and Radiance and Wisdom." In the incarnation the Son willingly and lovingly took on the human flesh derived from "a Virgin, Mary, Bearer of God, and was made man." The Word was "not external" to the humanity he had assumed. Rather, when the incarnate Son lived and ministered on earth, humanity and deity were both at work in an incomprehensible union. When Jesus healed the mother-in-law of Simon Peter, "He stretched forth His hand humanly, but He stopped the illness divinely."[48] When he healed the man born blind from birth, "human was the spittle which He gave forth from the flesh, but divinely did He open the eyes through the clay." At the raising of Lazarus, "he gave forth a human voice, as man; but divinely, as God, did He raise Lazarus from the dead."[49] Athanasius sees the Son's incarnate actions as manifesting the genuine union existing in his person between his humanity and his deity. If he grieved or expressed other human emotions, such was only proper. For "it became the Lord, in putting on human flesh, to put it on whole with the affections proper to it," though Athanasius is uncomfortable with the idea that Christ's human "affections" touched his deity.[50]

It is at Nicea in 325 CE that the first great ecumenical council, under the

---

48. Athanasius, *Four Discourses Against the Arians*, p. 411.
49. Athanasius, *Four Discourses Against the Arians*, p. 411.
50. Athanasius, *Four Discourses Against the Arians*, p. 411.

leadership of Athanasius, affirmed the eternal generation of the Son (against modalism). It also stated that the Son was *homoousios* or of the "same essence" or "being" as the Father (against Arianism and any type of ontological hierarchialism in the Godhead). The meaning of the *homoousion* would be the center of debate in Christian theology for the next fifty years.[51]

All three of the great Cappadocian fathers, Basil the Great (330-370 CE), Gregory of Nazianzus (329-390 CE), and Gregory of Nyssa (335-394 CE), were key contributors to the flowering of trinitarian reflection in the fourth century. The Eunomians particularly attracted their attention, a radical Arian group who prided themselves on their supposed ability to rationally plumb the depths of the divine nature. Eunomius and his followers especially relished utilizing syllogisms to seemingly demonstrate the incoherence of trinitarian ideas and formulations. The Cappadocians responded vigorously in their sermons, letters, and treatises.

Gregory of Nazianzus, the close friend and confidant of Basil, served for a short but extremely crucial period as bishop of Constantinople during the theologically heated era of the Arian controversy. It was during Gregory's episcopate in Constantinople in the latter stages of the fourth century that he preached a series of homilies attacking the rampant Arianism rumbling through the city.

In these sermons or "orations" Gregory centered his attention on the highly rationalistic Eunomians. The Eunomians seemed to believe that "anyone with an ounce of sense . . . would surely recognize that there was only one God, the Father. To predicate further personal distinctions within God's being was to speak incomprehensible gibberish. In fact, there was scant room in Eunomian thought for incomprehensibility or mystery of any sort."[52]

---

51. Cary notes that the Nicean *homoousios* should never be interpreted in a materialist sense, as though Father and Son share a common divine "stuff" out of which both are made. "That would make the divine essence or *ousia* into a kind of material out of which the Father and Son were both made — like two rings made of gold. In that case Arius would be right to object that the divine substance was divided, and the Father was lessened by giving birth to the Son. Not only that, the divine substance or *ousia* would be something other than Father and Son, a thing underlying them both and more fundamental than they are — as gold exists before the rings which are made out of it and could continue to exist even if the rings were melted down and destroyed. The general point is that the divine *ousia* cannot mean some fourth thing behind, beneath, or before Father, Son, and Holy Spirit" ("Historical Perspectives on Trinitarian Doctrine," p. 4).

52. Christopher A. Hall, *Reading Scripture with the Church Fathers* (Downers Grove: InterVarsity Press, 1998), p. 69.

In his theological orations Gregory defends the deity of both the Son and the Holy Spirit, proposing the idea of progressive revelation as a helpful concept in the substructure of trinitarian thought. "The Old Testament," Gregory writes, "proclaimed the Father openly, and the Son more obscurely. The New manifested the Son, and suggested the deity of the Spirit. Now the Spirit dwells among us, and supplies us with a clearer demonstration of himself."[53] Why such a slow, revelatory progression? ". . . [I]t was not safe, when the Godhead of the Father was not yet acknowledged, plainly to proclaim the Son; nor when that of the Son was not received, to burden us further (if I may use so bold an expression) with the Holy Ghost."[54]

Basil sprinkles a number of significant and insightful trinitarian insights throughout his voluminous correspondence.[55] In letter 189, for instance, Basil responds to Sabellians who accused him and other trinitarian theologians of "worshipping three gods." In response, Basil encourages his opponents to turn to the scriptures and to allow them "to arbitrate between us, and the doctrines of whichever side are found to be in harmony with the words of God, to that side will surely go the verdict of the truth."

He proceeds to defend the deity of the Holy Spirit. Basil reminds his correspondent that the character and activities of the Holy Spirit — "the good, the holy, and the eternal, the wise, the right, the supreme, the powerful" — are possessed and exercised in common with the Father and the Son. If so, Basil deduces, must not the Spirit possess the same nature as the Father and Son? "For," Basil writes, "all conceptions and terms proper to God are held of equal honor one with another, through the fact that there is no discrepancy in the signification of the subject." For instance, when "good" is applied to one member of the Trinity, it is not as though this designation is ever thought to apply only to this subject. Rather, terms such as "good," "wise," "powerful," and "just" apply to all the persons or subjects. Or, as Basil puts it, "whatever terms you use, the thing that is signified by them all is one."[56]

---

53. Gregory of Nazianzus, "The Fifth Theological Oration — On the Spirit," in *Christology of the Later Fathers,* ed. Edward R. Hardy (Philadelphia: Westminster Press, 1954), p. 207.

54. Gregory of Nazianzus, "The Fifth Theological Oration," p. 207.

55. Cf. particularly letters 8, 38, 52, 125, 189, 214, and 236 in Saint Basil, *Letters,* trans. Roy J. DeFerrari (Cambridge, Mass.: Harvard University Press, 1986).

56. Saint Basil, *Letters,* letter 189, p. 59.

Basil reinforces these ideas in his treatise *On the Holy Spirit*, where he develops his case for the Spirit's divinity by focusing on the work of the Spirit and the implications of this work for his person. That is, if the Spirit does the kinds of things only God can rightly do, he must share the divine nature with the Father and Son. In discussing the Spirit, Basil specifically asks, "What does the Spirit do?" "Resurrection from the dead is accomplished by the operation of the Spirit. . . . He gives us risen life, refashioning our souls in the spiritual life." If so, how can the Christian "be afraid of giving the Spirit too much honor? We should instead fear that even though we ascribe to Him the highest titles we can devise or our tongues pronounce, our ideas about Him might still fall short."[57]

In brief, all three Cappadocians contend that "all general terms (wisdom, power, goodness) refer to God in the singular: there is only one wisdom, one power, one goodness in God, not three."[58] In addition, the will and activity of God is also one. Here we see that all analogies drawn from human life ultimately break down when applied to trinitarian relationships. For example, Jane and John might share a common human nature but choose as individual persons to exercise their wills in opposition to one another. Their individuality as persons surely leaves the autonomous exercise of their wills as a genuine possibility. Not so with God. Although God's being is characterized by the hypostatic distinctions of Father, Son, and Spirit, all three persons are one in their will and activity. They are not autonomous persons in the modern nuance of "individual," each with its own separate "ego" and "center" of consciousness. Rather, they have always and will always purpose and operate with one will and action. They are one God, not three.[59]

What, however, of narratives in the gospels where Jesus clearly submits his will to the Father? One thinks of the struggle of Jesus in the garden of Gethsemane. Finally, after much struggle in prayer, Jesus submits his will to the Father. "Yet not what I will, but what you will" (Mark 14:36). Does not this indicate two wills, and if so, the lingering possibility of at least two gods? Eastern theology, rooted in the thought of the Cappadocians, has re-

57. Basil the Great, *On the Holy Spirit*, trans. David Anderson (Crestwood, N.Y.: St. Vladimir's Press, 1980), pp. 76-78.

58. Cary, "Historical Perspectives on Trinitarian Doctrine," p. 4.

59. Cary comments: ". . . God is *not* three persons in the modern sense of the word — for three distinct divine persons, with three distinct minds, wills and centers of consciousness, would surely be three Gods (just as the Cappadocians said)" (p. 5).

sponded with the distinction between *theologia,* "the doctrine of the nature of God in eternity, which focuses on the Trinity," and *oikonomia* or "economy," centered on the incarnation.[60] Thus, Jesus' human will is distinct from his divine will in the economy of the incarnation. In Gethsemane Jesus in obedience submits his will to the Father, while his divine will remains one with the Father's.

In the same manner, when Jesus speaks of the Father as being "greater than I," the reference is to the economy of the incarnation. The Father is indeed greater than the Son with reference to the Son's humanity. "Without this [key] distinction between *theologia* and *oikonomia* we would have to interpret the obedience of Christ to the Father as an indication that even in his divine being he was subordinate to the Father — and that would be the end of Nicene trinitarianism."[61] Again, in the Trinity we have one God, not three.

If so, we must exercise great care in asserting that the Cappadocians strongly affirmed the reality of a "social Trinity," simply because what we mean by "social" on a human level breaks down when speaking of the divine persons. Human social relationships, for instance, are characterized by separate individuals or social groups interacting with other individuals or groups. These interactions can demonstrate marked agreement and harmony. At other times, tensions and disagreements rise to the surface. Such is not the case within the Trinity itself. Here there is no possibility of disagreement or conflict, because all three are one in will and activity. Rather than accentuating the social Trinity, "the Cappadocians compared the Trinity to a society of three human beings precisely in order to show why the comparison breaks down — i.e. why the Father, Son and Holy Spirit are not three Gods," unlike Jane, John, and George, three human persons sharing a common human nature.[62]

Gregory of Nyssa, brother of Basil, was concerned to overturn the common misconception that the doctrine of the Trinity was essentially tritheism. In Gregory's treatise *On "Not Three Gods." To Ablabius,* Gregory analyzes the nature of God's unity grounded in the shared divinity of Father, Son, and Holy Spirit. The one *ousia* of Father, Son, and Spirit, Gregory contends, must never lead to the conclusion that the Trinity is in reality three gods. To simply affirm that Father, Son, and Spirit possess a common nature is not enough to

---

60. Cary, "Historical Perspectives on Trinitarian Doctrine," p. 8.
61. Cary, "Historical Perspectives on Trinitarian Doctrine," p. 8.
62. Cary, "Historical Perspectives on Trinitarian Doctrine," p. 6.

avoid tritheism, on at least two counts: first, a common nature can be shared by more than one individual. For example, the gods of the Greek pantheon were believed to share a common nature, and yet were clearly not one God.[63] Human beings share a common nature. Still, the Mary, Joe, or Sam who share that nature are unique, separate, individuals.

Second, the divine nature by definition ". . . cannot be named and is ineffable. We say that every name, whether invented by human custom or handed down by the scriptures, is indicative of our conceptions of the divine nature, but does not signify what that nature is in itself."[64] God's nature or essence remains "unlimited," "unnameable," "unspeakable," "incomprehensible," and "infinite." As "infinite," God's essence "is not limited in one respect while it is left unlimited in another, but infinity is free from limitation altogether. That therefore which is without limit is surely not limited by name."[65] We do know, however, that our understanding of God's nature cannot be drawn from human nature or pagan pantheons, both of which "possess one nature just as God is said to possess one nature, but are still counted as many 'men' or many 'gods.'"[66]

What knowledge we are to have of God, then, must come from God's operations. Or in Gregory's words, human reason can "perceive only the varied operations of the transcendent power, and fits its way of speaking of him to each of the operations made known to us."[67] Our understanding of God's divinity, then, does not refer to God's nature in itself, but as revealed in an operation *(energeia)* "which emanates from the divine nature, and therefore manifests the supracomprehensible divinity. The divine operations, because they come from the divine nature and make it manifest, enable us to infer the natural unity of the three divine persons because we see all three persons performing the same natural operation together."[68]

---

63. For an extremely helpful explanation of Gregory's argument to which we are indebted, cf. Kenneth Paul Wesche, "The Triadological Shaping of Latin and Greek Christology, Part II: The Greek Tradition," *Pro Ecclesia* 2, no. 1, pp. 85-89.

64. Gregory of Nyssa, *Quod Non Sint Tres Dii*, PG 45, col. 121 AB; quoted in Wesche, "The Triadological Shaping of Latin and Greek Christology," p. 87.

65. Gregory of Nyssa, On *"Not Three Gods." To Ablabius*, NPNF Second Series, vol. 5 (Peabody, Mass.: Hendrickson, 1994), p. 335.

66. Wesche, "The Triadological Shaping of Latin and Greek Christology," p. 87.

67. Gregory of Nyssa, *Quod Non Sint Tres Dii*, in On *"Not Three Gods,"* col. 121C; quoted in Wesche, p. 87.

68. Wesche, "The Triadological Shaping of Latin and Greek Christology," p. 87.

God has graciously chosen to reveal himself to us in his operations as Father, Son, and Holy Spirit. That is, the persons of the Trinity reveal God to us in an economic and undivided fashion. Our names for God come from God's operations. ". . . [A]s we perceive the varied operations of the power above us, we fashion our appellations from the several operations that are known to us."[69] Such is not the case with the divine nature itself. We do not learn from God's divine essence "that the Father does anything by Himself in which the Son does not work conjointly, or again that the Son does not work conjointly, or again that the Son has any special operation from the Holy Spirit."[70] Instead, "every operation which extends from God to the Creation, and is named according to our variable conceptions of it, has its origin in the Holy Spirit."[71] Wesche helpfully comments:

> These are not three separate actors, each one scheming against the other to effect his own agenda as one finds in the Olympian pantheon, nor is there one common operation performed independently by each of the Three as in the case, for example, of several human orators, or farmers, or shoemakers who each one perform the same activity, but independently of others; there is but one natural operation which all three persons perform, each in his own way, but in natural union with the others. There is accordingly identity of purpose, will and knowledge; the Son knows what the Father is doing because his action is the Father's action and it is the very action perfected by the Holy Spirit.[72]

Roughly three centuries after Gregory of Nyssa, John of Damascus (ca. 650 [or 675] to ca. 749 CE) added his own trinitarian reflections to the church's treasury, especially in regard to the Spirit's role in the Trinity. Phillip Cary notes that John's *Exact Exposition of the Orthodox Faith,* especially Book I, chapters 5-8, is "the most comprehensive brief (15 pp.) statement of Greek trinitarian doctrine."[73] The richness of John's trinitarian

---

69. Gregory of Nyssa, On *"Not Three Gods,"* p. 333.

70. Gregory of Nyssa, On *"Not Three Gods,"* p. 334.

71. Gregory of Nyssa, On *"Not Three Gods,"* p. 334.

72. Wesche, "The Triadological Shaping of Latin and Greek Christology," p. 88.

73. Phillip Cary, "The Logic of Trinitarian Doctrine," *Religious and Theological Studies Fellowship Bulletin* (September/October 1995): 7; cf. John of Damascus, *Exposition of the Orthodox Faith,* NPNF Second Series, vol. 9.

thoughts is difficult to capture in a short space. Among other things, John's work demonstrates how the church's understanding of the Holy Spirit had matured since Nicea (325 CE) and Constantinople (381 CE). Whereas the Spirit had appeared almost as a footnote to the creed of Nicea, John writes richly of the Spirit's person and work.

The Holy Spirit, "the Lord and Giver of Life . . . proceeds from the Father and rests in the Son." The Spirit is "the object of equal adoration and glorification with the Father and Son, since He is co-essential and co-eternal . . . authoritative, the fountain of wisdom, and life, and holiness." "[A]ll-ruling, all-effecting, all-powerful, of infinite power, Lord of all creation and not under any lord," the Spirit deifies but is not "deified," fills, but is not "filled," sanctifies, but is not "sanctified." As "the intercessor," the Spirit receives "the supplications of all: in all things like to the Father and Son: proceeding from the Father and communicated through the Son." The Spirit possesses his own "subsistence, existing in its own proper and peculiar subsistence, inseparable and indivisible from Father and Son, and possessing all the qualities that the Father and Son possess, save that of not being begotten or born."[74]

Key Latin Contributions

Ambrose, bishop of Milan in the latter years of the fourth century, has left us a significant body of trinitarian work. His *On the Christian Faith* and *On the Holy Spirit* are both indispensable works for understanding Latin trinitarian emphases and concerns, and can occasionally be found together as a single work with the title *De Trinitate*.

In *On the Holy Spirit* Ambrose observes that "the evident glory of the Godhead" is characterized by four chief "marks." God is "without sin," "forgives sin," "is not a creature but the Creator," and "does not give but receives worship."[75] Ambrose then argues that if these four marks set off God from all created reality and if the Holy Spirit is characterized by all four marks, the Spirit must be divine. For example, Ambrose believes that texts such as Job 33:4 ("The Spirit of God has made me") point to the Spirit as

74. John of Damascus, *Exposition of the Orthodox Faith*, chapter 8, p. 9.
75. Ambrose, *On the Holy Spirit*, NPNF Second Series, vol. 10 (Peabody, Mass.: Hendrickson, 1994), book 3, chapter 18, p. 154.

Creator and therefore God. "Let them," Ambrose writes, "therefore, either say what it is which has been created without the Father, Son, and Holy Spirit, or let them confess that the Spirit also is of one Godhead with the Father and the Son."[76]

On the Christian Faith more directly represents Ambrose's defense of the Trinity against its various opponents and deals with a number of key subjects and questions including: Arianism, the nature of the unity between the Father and Son, the deity of the Son, Christ's eternity, the nature of the divine generation, the various names of the Son, the goodness of the Son, the Son's omnipotence, and the purpose of the incarnation.

Throughout *On the Christian Faith* Ambrose exegetes a number of biblical passages, especially focusing on texts Arians employed in their argument that the Son was an exalted creature, but not God. In his summary of trinitarian faith Ambrose affirms that "God is One, neither dividing His Son from Him, as do the heathen, nor denying, with the Jews, that He was begotten of the Father before all worlds. . . ."[77] Ambrose denies Sabellius' position that personal distinctions within God's one nature do not exist. Ambrose warns his reader that one must not confound "the Father with the Word, and so" maintain "that Father and Son are one and the same Person." Nor does the Son come "into existence" for the first time in the "Virgin's womb," the position advocated by Photinus. As for Arius, his ideas concerning exalted creatures would inevitably lead to a belief in multiple gods. "God is One," Ambrose writes, and so is God's name. "Christ Himself, indeed, says: 'Go, ye, baptize the nations in the name of the Father, and of the Son, and of the Holy Spirit.'[78] In the *name*, mark you, not in the names."[79]

Hilary of Poitiers (*circa* 315-*circa* 367) was a man of keen theological insight and immense personal courage and integrity. Like other church fathers who defended the deity of the incarnate Son, Hilary suffered political retaliation from the Roman emperor Constantius II. Constantius, sympathetic to the Arian position, exiled Hilary from his Western episcopate in Poitiers to the East. Remarkably, it was in the Eastern Christian world, more particularly in Phrygia, that Hilary was first exposed to the Nicean

76. Ambrose, *On the Holy Spirit*, book 3, chapter 18, para. 140, p. 155.
77. Ambrose, *On the Christian Faith*, NPNF Second Series, vol. 10, book 1, chapter 1, para. 6, p. 202.
78. Matt. 28:19.
79. Ambrose, *On the Christian Faith*, book 1, chapter 1, paragraphs 6 and 8, pp. 202-3.

formulation *homoousion* that had been promulgated in 325 CE. It is in the East, then, that Hilary's trinitarian ideas fully mature with the writing of *The Trinity (De Trinitate)*.

Stephen McKenna describes Hilary's *The Trinity* as the earliest fully developed treatise by a Western Latin theologian on the topic of the Trinity. McKenna identifies Hilary as a "pioneer" who "had to coin many new words in order to express his thought accurately. Among the neologisms attributed to him are *abscissio, innascibilitas, ininitiabilis, supercreo,* and *consubsisto*. He also gave new meanings to words already in current use, as *sacramentum, dispensatio,* and *substitutio*."[80]

Later Latin theologians, Augustine, Leo, and Aquinas among them, praised Hilary's treatise and drew upon it themselves. McKenna comments that Aquinas "frequently appeals to it when settling disputes about the Trinity." In addition, it was Hilary who first "brought to the attention of the scholars of the Roman Empire in the West the vast theological riches of the Orient."[81]

Unfortunately, space limits us to only a very brief sampling of Hilary's thought, in this case a meditation on the Gospel of John. As Hilary meditated on John's prologue (John 1:1-14), his "fearful and anxious soul found greater hope than it had anticipated." As Hilary read he "received knowledge of the Father. What it [his soul] previously believed from natural reason about the eternity, infinity, and form of its Creator it now realizes as proper to the only-begotten God."

The prologue also makes clear that tritheism is not the belief of the Christian community regarding the Trinity. "It does not believe in many gods, because it hears of God from God, nor does it accept a difference in nature between God and God, because it learns that the God who is from God is full of grace and truth. . . ."[82]

Is there perhaps an "earlier and a later God from God"? Such could not be possible, because "God was with God in the beginning." As for the incarnation of the Son, "in order that the incarnate Word of God might not be anything else than God the Word, or anything else than flesh of our flesh, He dwelt among us, so that while He dwells He remains nothing else

80. Stephen McKenna, Introduction, Hilary of Poitiers, *On the Trinity*, Fathers of the Church, vol. 25 (Washington, D.C.: Catholic University of America Press, 1954), p. xiii.

81. McKenna, Introduction, Hilary of Poitiers, *On the Trinity*, p. xv.

82. Hilary of Poitiers, *On the Trinity*, chapter 1, p. 12.

than God." Yet while divine, "God became nothing else than flesh of our flesh. By humbling Himself to take our flesh He did not lose His own proper nature, because as the only-begotten of the Father He is full of grace and truth; He is perfect in His own and true in ours."[83]

Within a few lines Hilary addresses themes that will remain at the heart of the church's trinitarian reflection and creedal formulations: Three gods or one God? Does the generation of the Son entail a begetting in time? What do we mean by the generation or begetting of the Son? How is this begetting of God from God related to time? How is the incarnate Word related to the pre-incarnate Word? Is the incarnate Word still God? If so, has the Word genuinely become human? Human in what sense? Does the Word simply assume a human body, or also a human mind and will?

Hilary teaches that it is the second person of the Trinity who becomes incarnate, not the Godhead itself. Rightly so. For, as Thomas Oden indicates, if an undifferentiated God became human, "*if God were only one person*, it could not be proclaimed that God both sends and is sent; that God could be both lawgiver and obedient to law; that God could both make atonement and receive it; that God could both reject sin and offer sacrifice for it."[84]

It is in the *kenosis,* the self-emptying of the Son, that the triune rhythm and glory of the incarnation become manifest. Paul's words in Philippians 2:7 find their "most brilliant analysis," at least in Oden's estimation, in Hilary's exegesis. Hilary writes that "the emptying of the form is not the destruction of the nature, because He who empties Himself is not wanting in His own nature and He who receives remains." This is, indeed, mysterious, "because He empties Himself and receives Himself, but no destruction takes place so that He ceases to exist when He empties Himself or does not exist when He receives. Hence, the emptying brings it about that the form of a slave appears," but Christ as God continues to exist. What does this mean, "since it is only Christ who has received the form of a slave"?[85]

Augustine, the greatest of the Western church fathers, has made his own unique contribution to the trinitarian thought of the church, particu-

83. Hilary of Poitiers, *On the Trinity,* p. 12.

84. Thomas Oden, *The Word of Life* (San Francisco: Harper & Row, 1989), p. 77; cf. Hilary of Poitiers, *The Trinity,* NPNF Second Series, vol. 9 (Peabody, Mass.: Hendrickson, 1994), 9.38-42, pp. 167-70.

85. Hilary of Poitiers, *On the Trinity,* 9.44, pp. 334-35; quoted in Oden, *The Word of Life,* p. 80.

larly in the West. Thomas Marsh summarizes Augustine's aims in his monumental work, *The Trinity*, as fourfold: (1) "to state and explain" the church's "basic" doctrine of the Trinity; (2) to demonstrate that the doctrine of the Trinity as taught by the church is firmly grounded in the Scripture; (3) "to work out the peculiar rules of human language and logic" that "must be observed" if the church is to speak of the Triune God "correctly"; (4) "to attempt to discover in the highest form of creation immediately known to us, the human mind or spirit, vestiges of the Triune God who is its Origin and Creator."[86]

Certain interpreters of Augustine's thought, such as Marsh and Colin Gunton, are convinced that Augustine has erred in grounding his thought on the Trinity in the unity of the divine substance. Marsh, for instance, believes that Augustine has abandoned the earlier Latin tradition's "strong sense of the divine monarchy — the one God is first and foremost the Father," instead understanding the "one God to mean the divine substance or nature which *then* is verified in Father, Son and Holy Spirit."[87] The unfortunate result, Marsh contends, is that Augustine ends up removing "the concept of *taxis* or order from its central place in the traditional understanding of the Triad." By "doing so, [Augustine] has separated the concepts of substance and person . . . in giving primacy to the former he has, unwittingly to be sure, introduced an *impersonal* concept of God."[88]

Gunton voices a similar criticism, writing that Augustine "either did not understand the trinitarian theology of his predecessors, both East and West, or looked at their work with spectacles so strongly tinted with neoplatonic assumptions that they have distorted his work."[89] In Gunton's interpretation, the Cappadocians more wisely perceived the relations between Father, Son, and Spirit as rooted in the ontology of God. That is, the divine being itself is ontologically relational. There is no divine substance or essence behind, preceding, or supporting the hypostatic relations. "For them, the three persons are what they are in their relations, and therefore the relations qualify them ontologically, in terms of what they are."[90]

---

86. Thomas Marsh, *The Triune God: A Biblical, Historical, and Theological Study* (Mystic, Conn.: Twenty-Third Publications, 1994), p. 131.

87. Marsh, *The Triune God*, p. 132.

88. Marsh, *The Triune God*, p. 132.

89. Colin Gunton, *The Promise of Trinitarian Theology* (Edinburgh: T. & T. Clark, 1991), pp. 38-39.

90. Gunton, *The Promise of Trinitarian Theology*, p. 41.

Augustine errs, Gunton believes, by viewing a "relation as a logical rather than an ontological predicate. . . ."[91] The unfortunate result is that "he is precluded from being able to make claims about the being of the *particular* persons, who, because they lack distinguishable identity tend to disappear into the all-embracing oneness of God."[92] Augustine's analogies of the Trinity, Gunton argues, can be more readily traced "to Neoplatonic philosophy than to the triune economy, and . . . the outcome is . . . a view of an unknown substance *supporting* the three persons rather than *being constituted* by their relatedness."[93]

Other scholars remain unconvinced by interpretations of Augustine such as those offered by Marsh and Gunton. Phillip Cary, for example, speaks of the tendency of mistakes in scholarship to "sometimes acquire a life of their own as one scholar after another repeats an erroneous opinion without troubling to do a careful reading of the original sources." Cary believes "two such mistakes in the history of trinitarian doctrine are (1) that the Cappadocians had a social doctrine of the Trinity and (2) that Augustine, in contrast to the Cappadocians, 'started with' the unity of the divine essence rather than the distinction of the three persons."[94] In Cary's perspective, this "is simply not an accurate account of the shape of Augustine's trinitarian inquiries." Interestingly, Cary refers to the very same sections of Augustine's *On the Trinity* that Marsh criticizes.[95]

Cary, contra Marsh and Gunton, argues that Augustine actually builds on the position of the Cappadocians, rather than ignoring or dismissing it. "Augustine begins where the Cappadocians leave off: accepting their answer to the question 'why not three gods?' he proceeds to ask 'three *what?*' His concern is to elaborate the distinctions between the three on the assumption that they are one God. Augustine never uses the divine essence *per se* as his starting point."[96]

In this short essay we can only mention the current debate on Augustine and the Trinity. The fair and wise resolution of the debate, though, surely will depend on a thorough grounding in Augustine's trinitarian

91. Gunton, *The Promise of Trinitarian Theology,* p. 41.
92. Gunton, *The Promise of Trinitarian Theology,* p. 42.
93. Gunton, *The Promise of Trinitarian Theology,* pp. 42-43.
94. Cary, "Historical Perspectives on Trinitarian Doctrine," p. 9.
95. Sections 1.4 and 1.7.
96. Cary, "Historical Perspectives on Trinitarian Doctrine," p. 9.

thought, amply illustrated in *The Trinity,* but also available in many of his other theological treatises and sermons.[97]

Phillip Cary has identified seven key propositions of trinitarian theology. Indeed, Cary argues that these seven propositions demonstrate that trinitarian language can be summarized without employing "abstract or unbiblical language."[98] The first three propositions "confess the name of the triune God." That is, (1) the Father is God. (2) The Son is God. (3) The Holy Spirit is God. The next three propositions "indicate that these are not just three names for the same thing. . . ." (4) The Father is not the Son. (5) The Son is not the Spirit. (6) The Holy Spirit is not the Father. Finally, Cary lists the "clincher, which gives the doctrine its distinctive logic": (7) There is only one God. "These seven propositions are sufficient to formulate the doctrine of the Trinity — to give the bare bones of what the doctrine says and lay out its basic logical structure. The logical peculiarities of the doctrine arise from the interaction of these seven propositions."[99]

Augustine himself writes that there "is the Father and the Son and the Holy Spirit — each one of these is God, and all of them together are one God; each of these is a full substance and all together are one substance."[100] He then clearly distinguishes between the three persons, while affirming that they "have the same eternal nature, the same unchangeableness, the same majesty, the same power." Perhaps surprisingly, in light of the current debate, Augustine proceeds to locate the unity of the persons, not in the divine essence, but in the Father. "In the Father there is unity. . . . And the three are all one because of the Father, all equal because of the Son, and all in harmony because of the Holy Spirit."[101]

In Augustine's second sermon in the series "Of the Words of St. Matthew's gospel, chap. 3:13, 'Then Jesus cometh from Galilee to the Jordan

97. Trinitarian comments and analysis occur in Augustine's *Sermons for Christmas and Epiphany, Enchiridion, Faith, Hope and Charity, Confessions, Letters, On Christian Teaching, City of God, Faith and the Creed, Of the Morals of the Catholic Church, Reply to Faustus the Manichaean, On the Merits and Forgiveness of Sins, On the Baptism of Infants, On Rebuke and Grace, On the Predestination of the Saints, On the Gift of Perseverance, On the Spirit and the Letter, On the Soul and Its Origin, The Harmony of the Gospels,* and *Sermons on Selected Lessons of the New Testament.*

98. Phillip Cary, "The Logic of Trinitarian Doctrine [Part I]," p. 2.

99. Cary, "The Logic of Trinitarian Doctrine," p. 2.

100. Augustine, *On Christian Teaching* (Oxford: Oxford University Press, 1997), p. 10.

101. Augustine, *On Christian Teaching,* p. 10.

unto John, to be baptized of Him.' Concerning the Trinity," we have Augustine's own summary of his much longer work, *The Trinity* or *On the Trinity*. This might well be the place to begin an exploration of the basic principles underlying Augustine's trinitarian thought. In the sermon he sets out to address a number of important questions:

1. Does the Father ever act separately from the Son? Or the Son from the Father? Augustine's answer is no. From Augustine's insistence on the inseparable nature of the work of the Father and the Son, a second key question flows.
2. If the Father does nothing apart from the Son and vice versa, was the Father "born of the Virgin Mary"? Did he suffer under Pontius Pilate? Did he rise again from the dead and ascend to heaven? Augustine responds "no," well aware of the patripassian heresy. A third question quickly follows.
3. If the work of the Father and the Son is not identical, in what sense can we say that it is inseparable? Augustine answers that, "The Son indeed and not the Father was born of the Virgin Mary; but this very birth of the Son, and not of the Father, was the work of both the Father and the Son. The Father did not rise again, but the Son, yet the resurrection of the Son was the work of the Father and the Son."[102]

Augustine rightly insists that all trinitarian theology must arise from a heart and mind trained in humility. Trinitarian reflection can only blossom in a person who realizes the enormity of what is being attempted and our place before God. Humans can only safely speak of God from their knees. Augustine urges us to "remember who we are, and of Whom we speak. Let this and that, or whatever appertains to the nature of God, be with a pious faith embraced, with a holy respect entertained. . . . For it is not of such a nature as it can ascend into the heart of man; but the heart of man must itself ascend to it."[103]

How, in fact, can human beings adequately speak of God? The subject is too high. "For if you have been able to comprehend what you would say,

---

102. Augustine, *Sermons on Selected Lessons of the New Testament*, Sermon 2, "Of the Words of St. Matthew's gospel, chap. 3:13, 'Then Jesus cometh from Galilee to the Jordan unto John, to be baptized of Him.' Concerning the Trinity," trans. R. G. MacMullen, NPNF First Series, vol. 6 (Peabody, Mass.: Hendrickson, 1994), p. 261.

103. Augustine, *Sermons*, p. 262.

it is not God; if you have been able to comprehend it, you have comprehended something else instead of God. If you have been able to comprehend Him as you think, by so thinking you have deceived yourself."[104]

What, then, is one to do? Augustine counsels his reader to search for an analogy on a more attainable, humble plane, a "resemblance" among God's creation. "You were speaking of the Trinity of Majesty ineffable, and because you did fail in contemplating the Divine Nature, and with becoming humility did confess your infirmity, you did come down to human nature; pursue your inquiry there."[105]

How so? By remembering that humanity has been made in the image of God. "For God made man after His own image and likeness. Search then in thine own self, if haply the image of the Trinity bear not some vestige of the Trinity. And what is this image?"[106] Augustine directs his listeners to the human mind, the "inner man." Are there clues in the human mind, tracks of the divine, that might lead us to more clearly understand the reality of the Father, Son, and Holy Spirit?

In his famous construction, Augustine focuses on the memory, the understanding, and the will. The memory retains, but only through the operation of the understanding and the intent of the will to do so. "Memory," Augustine writes, "is the name of one only of those three, yet all the three concurred in producing the name of this single one of the three. The single word 'memory' could not be expressed, but by the operation of the will, and the understanding, and the memory." In turn, "the single word 'understanding' could not be expressed, but by the operation of the memory, the will, and the understanding." Likewise, "the single word 'will' could not be expressed, but by the operation of the memory and the understanding and the will."[107] And yet the word "memory" in and of itself has reference only to itself, and the same is also true of "understanding" and "will."

Augustine refrains from trying to identify the memory, understanding, or will with a specific person of the Trinity, counseling us to "leave somewhat to meditation and to silence." Instead, "believe that the Father, Son, and Holy Spirit may be exhibited separately, by certain visible sym-

104. Augustine, *Sermons*, p. 263.
105. Augustine, *Sermons*, p. 263.
106. Augustine, *Sermons*, p. 263.
107. Augustine, *Sermons*, p. 265.

bols, by certain forms borrowed from the creatures, and still their operations be inseparable."

Memory, will, and understanding seem to operate in this very fashion. Beware, though, of thinking that these analogies "are in any sort to be equaled with the Holy Trinity, to be squared after an analogy; that is, a kind of exact rule of comparison."[108] "We can know what is in us, but what is in Him who made you, whatever it be, how can you know? And if you shall be ever able, you are not able yet. And even when you shall be able, will you be able so to know God, as He knows Himself?"[109]

The acuity and agility of Augustine's mind, demonstrated as he grapples with trinitarian mysteries, has been acknowledged by his friends and foes, past and present. For Augustine, however, as for all the fathers, spiritual insight and holiness of life were inextricably linked. Theology was to be practiced in both the mind and heart; a diseased life would lead to a diseased theology. The fathers believed the opposite was also true; a life filled with the presence of Christ would surely affect the life of the mind and the intellect's ability to reason well and humbly. Holy character is demanded if holy things are to be understood and interpreted well.

In speaking of the relationship between Father and Son, Augustine comments that "seeing [that] this is a great mystery, *our conduct must be fashioned, that it may be comprehended. For to the unworthy is it closed up; it is opened to those who are meet for it.*" To seek after truth is for those who call upon the Lord, knocking with their lives. "*It is the life which knocks, it is to the life that it is opened. The seeking is with the heart, the asking is with the heart, the knocking is with the heart, the opening is to the heart*" (our emphasis).[110]

> *As with Augustine and the other patristic contributors we must acknowledge our dependence on the Trinity, God, to reveal himself to us. As we continue to study we also continue to seek the revelation of the Lord to our humble hearts and minds.*

108. Augustine, *Sermons*, p. 265.
109. Augustine, *Sermons*, p. 266.
110. Augustine, *Sermons,* Sermon 41, "On the Words of the Gospel, Matt. 22:42, Where the Lord asks the Jews whose son they said David was," p. 398.

2. The Trinity: Medieval, Reformation, and Modern Contributions

Early Medieval Contributions

Christian reflection on the triunity of God declined in creativity and depth after the great achievements of the patristic era which ended around 500 to 600 CE. Many theologians and church leaders in the Latin West regarded Augustine's constructive proposals — especially *De Trinitate* — the final word on the subject. That is not to say that no Western Christian thinkers added to the Augustinian synthesis. Boethius (d. *circa* 525) was one of the most influential thinkers of the early medieval period and wrote at least four philosophical-theological treatises on the doctrines of the Trinity and person of Jesus Christ. Best known for his influential book *On the Consolation of Philosophy,* the great Roman philosopher-statesman was also a major interpreter of the Augustinian tradition of trinitarian thought who sought to use Aristotelian categories to explain it. In at least one area Boethius seemed to diverge from Augustine's strong emphasis on the unity of the Trinity. At least his definition of "person" as an "individual substance of a rational nature" seemed to require a greater distinction between Father, Son, and Holy Spirit than Augustine's theology allowed.

Boethius provides a good example of a trend in theology in the Latin West throughout the post-Augustinian, medieval era that also helped set the stage for the reformations of the sixteenth century. Without rejecting biblical exegesis as a basis for doctrinal formulation and defense, Boethius and others like him tended to make greater use of speculation than did the earliest church fathers. The medieval mind of the Latin West made little distinction between philosophy and theology. Scripture, Plato, Aristotle, and subtle logical reasoning all played significant if not equal roles in developing explanations and defenses of doctrines such as the Trinity and person of Christ. In the process, however, very little was added to the great tradition of trinitarian thought that seemed to reach its pinnacle with the Cappadocian fathers in the East and Augustine in the West. Between them and the medieval scholastic renaissance of the twelfth and thirteenth centuries very little was added to that tradition other than Boethius' "new and unaccustomed words" and definitions of familiar terms.

Without any doubt the greatest controversy over the doctrine of the Trinity during the early medieval period (approximately 500 to 1000 CE) was the so-called "*filioque* controversy" that eventually contributed to the great schism between the Eastern and Western halves of Christendom. The habit of adding the Latin word *filioque* ("and the Son") to the Nicene (Niceno-Constantinopolitan) Creed of 381 gradually became accepted practice in Western monasteries and was justified on the basis of Augustine's doctrine of the Trinity, in which the Holy Spirit is distinguished from the Father and Son by "procession" or "spiration" from both of them. Exactly how the phrase "and the Son" entered into the creed in the West is unknown, but it may have happened first in Spain around the sixth century. Monks arriving on pilgrimage in Palestine (where Greek-speaking Byzantine Christians tended to be more numerous and dominant) recited the creed saying that "the Spirit proceeds from the Father *and the Son.*" The Byzantine monks and priests objected to this interpolation on the grounds that it violated the integrity of the creed which did not originally contain the phrase "and the Son" *(filioque)* and that it subordinated the Holy Spirit to the Son. Over a period of a few centuries the argument over this one Latin phrase blew up into a cause of mutual excommunication between the bishops of the East and the bishops of the West. Emperors on both sides became involved, as did patriarchs and popes. Finally, in 1054 the two sides officially excommunicated one another. Of course there were many other factors that contributed to the schism that took place in the great cathedral of Byzantium (Istanbul, Constantinople), but for almost one thousand years theologians and churchmen of both sides have repeatedly pointed to the *filioque* clause as a major one.

If Boethius represents the overall tenor and approach of Western Latin theology in the early medieval period, the Byzantine patriarch Photius (d. *circa* 897) well represents Eastern trinitarian thought during the same general epoch. Like Boethius, Photius was a great scholar who has been called a "learned humanist" because he was steeped in the philosophy and literature of classical culture as well as in the biblical and patristic sources of Christian thought. Unlike Boethius, Photius was a bishop who was elevated to the high office of patriarch of Constantinople (Byzantium) by the Eastern emperor. Photius took on as a special task defeat of the infamous *filioque* clause in the Latin version of the Nicene Creed. In his *Mystagogia Spiritus Sancti* (extant in Latin but never fully translated into English) Photius offered the Eastern Church's definitive arguments against the Western doctrine of the Trinity as he saw it implied by the *filioque* clause. Besides arguing that *filioque* is illegitimate because it is an innovation introduced non-ecumenically by the West (supported only by Western emperors and popes), Photius also argued that neither Scripture nor the church fathers (before Augustine, at least) lend any support to belief in the Holy Spirit's procession from the Son: ". . . neither in the divine words of Scripture nor in the human words of the holy Fathers was it ever verbally enunciated that the Spirit proceeds from the Son."[1] More subtle are Photius' dialectical arguments against the *filioque* concept. Photius attempted to show that confession of the Spirit's procession from both the Father and the Son (eternally, within the Godhead itself) raises more questions than it answers and is actually evidence of a subordination of the Holy Spirit to the Son within the immanent Trinity. In keeping with the historic position of the Eastern church fathers at least since the Cappadocians, Photius averred that the only orthodox doctrine of the eternal triune being of God is one that sees the Father as the "fount of the divinity" of both the Son and the Spirit, who are eternally generated and proceed from the Father respectively. The Latin West rejected Photius' arguments while the East accepted them.[2]

In general, then, the second half of the first millennium of Christian theological reflection lacked great creative vigor and depth especially in the area of the doctrine of the Trinity. No theologian rose to the level of the Cappadocian fathers Basil and the two Gregories or to Augustine's height. Discussion focused on and revolved around subtle points of interpretation

---

1. Edmund J. Fortman, *The Triune God: A Historical Study of the Doctrine of the Trinity* (London: Hutchinson & Co., 1972), p. 94.

2. See Richard S. Haugh, *Photius and the Carolingians: The Trinitarian Controversy* (Belmont, Mass.: Nordland Publishing Co., 1975).

of key terms such as *prosopa* and *persona* and *filioque*. Political tensions between leaders of the Latin West and Greek East often overshadowed theological reflection and creativity. The doctrine of the Trinity languished to a certain extent as many Christian thinkers considered it all but fully settled and contented themselves with either repeating past formulations or putting the finishing touches on it through dialectical argumentation and speculation. Such was the case until the so-called medieval renaissance of philosophy and theology that began especially in the twelfth century and reached its height in the thirteenth century when the full flowering of scholasticism breathed some new life into Christian trinitarian thought.

High and Late Medieval Contributions

A major project of medieval European Christian thinkers was to explore the logical status of Christian dogmas such as the Trinity and incarnation. These scholastic thinkers often barely distinguished between theology and philosophy, and they tended to assume that if Christian theological beliefs were true their logical necessity could be demonstrated. There were exceptions to this assumption, of course, and right at the beginning of the medieval renaissance of Christian thought two outstanding Latin Christian intellectuals disagreed radically about this issue. The great Anselm of Canterbury (d. 1109) sought to show the logical necessity of Christian dogmas while his younger counterpart Peter Abelard (d. 1142) was less sanguine about the ability of the human mind conclusively to prove all Christian doctrines. Nevertheless, even Abelard linked faith and reason closely together even as he affirmed that reason alone could never completely replace faith.

For these and later medieval Latin Christian thinkers, such as Thomas Aquinas (d. 1274), the doctrine of the Trinity provided wonderful grist for the philosophical-theological speculative mill. While almost all of them assumed the authority of the early church's conciliar declarations regarding the person of Christ (one person with two natures) and the Trinity (three persons sharing one substance) they also believed that such newly discovered intellectual resources as Aristotle's philosophy could aid Christians in solving some of the problems that had arisen in dialogues and debates between Catholics, Moslems, and Jews in North Africa and Spain. Mystically inclined Christian thinkers such as Joachim of Fiore (sometimes spelled

"Flora") (d. 1202) sought to link trinitarian dogma with the flow of history and inner experiences of God without rejecting rigorous intellectual wrestling with the dogma. Perhaps the most creative and influential of all the medieval Catholic trinitarian thinkers was Richard of St. Victor (d. 1173), who provided a new way of thinking about the unity of the trinitarian persons that some during his own lifetime and since have considered almost heretical but is widely accepted in the modern world of Christian trinitarian reflection. Two ecumenical councils that dealt with the Trinity met in the Latin West (not recognized by the Greek East) during the high middle ages: the Fourth Lateran Council (1215) and the Council of Florence (1438-1445). Both helped settle some debates over the details of the doctrine of the Trinity.

Overall and in general the high medieval era in Europe was not a time of great creativity with regard to trinitarian reflection, but it was a time when certain Christian thinkers returned to rigorous examination and construction of the doctrine of the Trinity using the tools of divine revelation and human reason. What follows here will be a few thumbnail sketches of some of the major contributors to the church's thinking about the mystery of God's triunity.

Anselm of Canterbury is often considered one of the premier Christian thinkers of the European middle ages and is best known in modern times for his formulations of the so-called "ontological argument" for the existence of God. He is also remembered for providing a "proof" of the dogma of the two natures of Christ (hypostatic union) in his book *Cur Deus Homo? (Why God Became Man)* and in the process constructing a new model of the atonement that came to be known as the "Satisfaction Theory." In various works in Latin (not all translated into English) Anselm attempted to correct heresies about the Trinity and shed some rational light on the mystery. His best-known trinitarian books include *De fide Trinitatis* (The trinitarian faith), *De processions Spiritus Sancti contra Graecos* (The procession of the Holy Spirit against the Greeks), and *Monologion.*

Anselm was greatly influenced by Augustine and stands squarely in the "line" of Augustinian theology that tended to dominate Latin Christian thought as well as that of many of the later Protestant reformers. Augustine was influenced by Platonic thought, which inclined his trinitarian reflections in the direction of the unity of the Godhead. For him, the Holy Spirit is the third "person" of the Trinity as the "bond of love" that unites

Father and Son and proceeds from both of them. Advocates and defenders of the *filioque* clause in the Latin Nicene Creed could point back to Augustine's formulations in order to justify the phrase's addition to the creed on theological grounds. Anselm picked up this Augustinian tradition of trinitarian reflection and added to it a decidedly scholastic "spin." That is, Anselm used logic to demonstrate not only the compatibility of the mystery of the Trinity (and other dogmas of Christianity) with reason but also its logical necessity. In brief, according to Anselm in his *Monologion,* the divine creator of all must necessarily be *both* perfectly unified in himself as one essence or substance *and* possess three (and no more than three) distinct relations within himself. This argument of Anselm's represents a scholastic expression and defense of Augustine's famous "psychological analogy" for the triunity of God. The "Supreme Spirit" (Father) must of necessity be intellectual (to have created a world) and that eternally. This Supreme Spirit eternally expresses himself and this eternal self-expression is his Word (Son) which belongs to his essence, but is not strictly identical with him because he is begotten (generated) as thought is begotten by intellect. Father and Son, then, are related as mind and thought are related. They are strictly consubstantial (one in essence and being), but distinct as to modality or relation. Two such relations within one essential, intellectual being must have a third as the love that binds them together and that is the Holy Spirit — the third relation within the divine essence that proceeds eternally from both the Father and the Son.[3]

Anselm's argumentation for the Augustinian vision of the Trinity along essentialist-intellectual lines is extremely subtle, and many modern readers find that it makes conceptual leaps that seem contrived. Whether Anselm was correct in believing that the Trinity can be proven logically (beginning with belief in a single Supreme Spirit who is creator of everything) is debatable. What is important for the history of the doctrine of the Trinity is his reinforcing of the Augustinian psychological model of the Trinity in which the divine being is assumed to be intellectual in nature and the distinctions between the three persons of the one divine being are reduced to relations of origin (generation and procession from each other in terms of mental activity). Some critics of the Augustinian-Anselmian psychological model of the Trinity have averred that it necessarily implies

3. Anselm, *Saint Anselm: Basic Writings,* trans. S. N. Deane (La Salle, Ill.: Open Court Publishing Co., 1962), chapters 30-63, pp. 91-127.

a modalistic vision of the Trinity and reduces the Holy Spirit to a kind of "glue" between Father and Son. That is, it may de-personalize the Holy Spirit, justifying reference to the third person of the Trinity as "It."[4] Anselm's subtle dialectical and psychological reflections on the Trinity heavily influenced the medieval Catholic Church's dogmatic defenses of the Trinity including *filioque* as formulated officially at two councils: Lateran IV in 1215 and Florence in 1438-1445. The latter council raised to dogmatic status one of Anselm's contributions — the conclusion that "everything in God is identical except where opposed relations (as in Father, Son, and Holy Spirit) stand in the way of identity."[5] By "opposed relations" Anselm and the council meant "relations of origin" so that the only thing that makes the Son not the Father is that he is begotten (generated) by him and the only thing that makes the Holy Spirit not the Father or the Son is that he proceeds from both of them. Thus, if the Spirit did not proceed from the Son *(filioque)* he would be strictly identical with the Son in every way or else he would be "another Son" which would imply multiplicity within the Trinity and disrupt the simplicity of the divine essence (tritheism).

Richard of St. Victor, although a scholastic medieval theologian, was less concerned than Anselm with logical, deductive proofs of the dogmas of the church such as the Trinity. Like Anselm he was impressed with and influenced by Augustine, but unlike Anselm he picked up on and made use of a *personalist* strand in Augustine's trinitarian theology that allowed him to emphasize the distinctness of the three persons of Father, Son, and Holy Spirit. Richard was also more mystical than most scholastics and more inclined toward use of spirituality in theology. He was not satisfied with the widely accepted psychological model of the Trinity and wanted to show how the three persons could be genuinely distinct persons and yet be one God. Richard's legacy to the history of the doctrine of the Trinity lies in the development over time of a so-called "social analogy" or "social model" of the Trinity in the West[6] that is in many ways closer to the Greek idea of the Trinity (especially as expressed in the Cappadocian fathers of the fourth

---

4. Jürgen Moltmann, *The Trinity and the Kingdom: The Doctrine of God*, trans. Margaret Kohl (San Francisco: Harper & Row, 1981) and *The Spirit of Life: A Universal Affirmation*, trans. Margaret Kohl (Minneapolis: Fortress Press, 1992).

5. Fortman, *The Triune God*, p. 227.

6. See Leonard Hodgson, *The Doctrine of the Trinity* (New York: Charles Scribner's Sons, 1944).

century). Richard of St. Victor's subtle corrections and adjustments to the Anselmian version of the Augustinian psychological model of the Trinity have been rediscovered and used in the twentieth century with the rise to prominence, especially among certain Protestants, of the social model of divine love.

Richard of St. Victor was a disciple of the lesser-known Hugh of St. Victor (d. 1141), who attempted to show compatibility between scholastic theology and mystical theology. Although Hugh's trinitarian thought is in many ways similar to Anselm's and certainly counts as an example of the Augustinian psychological model because it compares the Trinity with the human soul (intellectually conceived as mind or thought), it included an element that helped contribute to a greater emphasis on the distinctness of the three persons of the Godhead. That element is the doctrine of the "divine appropriations" or "divine attributions." Certainly Hugh was not the first Christian thinker to suggest the idea that certain acts or operations of God are especially connected at least in human thought with certain persons, but he emphasized this idea in a way that influenced his disciple Richard of St. Victor to develop further the distinctness of the persons. The doctrine of "appropriations" or "attributions" (found especially in Hugh's influential Latin work *De sacramentis fidei Christianae*) means that at least in human reflection upon the divine Trinity it is proper to think and speak of the Father as especially involved in, for example, the work of creation while thinking and speaking of the Son as especially involved in redemption. This is to "appropriate" or "attribute" these works especially to one of the three divine persons while acknowledging the principle laid down by the early church fathers that "operations of the three persons of the Trinity toward what is outside of the Trinity are indivisible" *(opera trinitatis ad extra indivisa sunt)*. The functions of the Trinity must be wholly unified so that all three persons are involved in each, but individual persons of the Trinity may be *said to be* especially at work in certain activities of creation, redemption, and sanctification. This principle of appropriation-attribution connects with spiritual life because one may contemplate the grace of a particular person of the Trinity and praise him for it without implying any separation of the being of God.

Richard of St. Victor picked up on Hugh's latent emphasis on the distinctiveness of the three persons and took it further without in any way implying (as some have supposed) tritheism (belief in three gods). Richard's most important and influential book is his *De Trinitate*, which has never been translated wholly into modern English. Rather than beginning with the typical Augustinian starting point of emphasizing the divine unity of essence and seeking to explain how there can be multiplicity within it, Richard begins with the persons of Father, Son, and Holy Spirit and with human persons in community and attempts to demonstrate how unity of essence is required by perfect love between persons. In this process the Victorine proposed a new definition of "person" as "an incommunicable existence of the divine nature." There must be three such "persons" in God, Richard argued, if God is love as Scripture avers. That is because perfect love is always directed toward what is distinct from and in some sense outside the self. Self-love is imperfect love. God's love must be perfect *and* not in any way dependent upon the creation. Thus, God's love must be other-directed within God himself. This is why there must be at least two persons (incommunicable existents) within God: the lover and the beloved. But might there be only two, then, and if so why a Trinity and not a "Binity"? Richard's response is ingenious and hotly debated. He argued that love between two is less perfect than among three. There is always a tinge of selfishness in the mutual love of only two persons and that only when a third belongs to the circle of love is love perfected, for "in mutual love that is very fervent there is nothing rarer, nothing more excellent than that you wish another to be equally loved by him whom you love supremely and by whom you are loved supremely." Richard concluded that perfect love such as God is "cannot be had without a Trinity of persons."[7]

Some fairly obvious questions linger over and around Richard of St. Victor's incipient social model of the Trinity. Why only three and not four? Would not love be even more perfect among four or more than among only three? Also, how are three incommunicable existents (persons), however locked in mutual love, really one divine substance or essence? Does not this Victorine social model inevitably lead to tritheism? Similar questions may be raised about Anselm's (or others') Augustinian psychological analogies of the Trinity insofar as they stress the unity of the divine substance in terms of one intellectual essence. How are memory, understanding, and will truly three "persons"? How does this escape Sabellianism or modalism? And, why insist that intellect requires three and only three mutually related aspects? Why not throw into the equation others such as "affections" or "hope," etc.? In any case, Richard's social model does not seem

7. Fortman, *The Triune God*, p. 193.

any more flawed as a complete account of the triune being of God than Anselm's psychological model. Many Christian theologians have wondered whether one model can ever suffice for giving as complete an account as possible of the Trinity. Might they be complementary rather than competitive?

Two lesser medieval theologians whose trinitarian reflections were judged heretical (rightly or wrongly) because they verged too close to or fell absolutely into either Sabellianism (modalism) or tritheism were Peter Abelard and Joachim of Fiore. These two medieval Christian thinkers of the Latin West well represent opposite tendencies in maverick trinitarian thought. Both were condemned as heretics in part due to their formulations of the doctrine of the Trinity, and both have been rehabilitated by later generations of Christians who are either more generous or less concerned with precise orthodoxy or both. Neither Abelard nor Joachim intended to be heretical, and if one necessary criterion of true heresy is *obstinacy in error* — as some Catholic and Orthodox theologians have argued — then they were not really heretics. Both were sufficiently ambiguous that their exact beliefs are difficult to determine.

Peter Abelard was a maverick philosopher and theologian of Paris around the time of Anselm. He is often considered a precursor of nominalism because he questioned the objective reality of universals such as "redness" and "human nature" and emphasized the ontological priority of individual existing things or abstractions. He is also remembered for his misfortunes recounted in some detail in his autobiography and reflected in his love correspondence with Heloise, whose uncle had Abelard castrated by thugs because the two had been secretly married. In theology Abelard is best known for raising questions about the alleged consensus of Christian doctrine in his dialectical book *Sic et Non* ("Yes and No"), where he juxtaposed opposite conclusions about dogmatic issues in the tradition going back to the church fathers. In his book *Tractatus de Unitate et Trinitate Divina* the brilliant but unfortunate Parisian teacher seemed to verge too close to Sabellianism or modalism when he compared the Trinity to a brass seal (the metal, the seal, its impression in wax) and wrote that "God is three persons in such a way as if we said that the divine substance is powerful, wise, and good."[8] Whether Abelard's doctrine of the Trinity is any more modalistic than Augustine's or Anselm's is debatable, but at the very

8. Fortman, *The Triune God*, p. 177.

least one must say that it is confused and confusing. The Council of Soissons (actually a synod of bishops) in 1121 condemned the book as "Sabellian" and burned it publicly. Abelard wrote an apology in which he retracted any unintentional heresies into which he may have fallen in that book and others and avoided being burned at the stake. However, his reputation as a rebel against authority (earned perhaps merely for questioning the standard expressions of church dogma and pointing out inconsistencies in it) plagued him throughout his life and he died on a journey to Rome to appeal a condemnation brought against him by his nemesis Bernard of Clairvaux.

Opposite Abelard's allegedly modalistic trinitarian reflections were those of the great Italian monastic mystic Joachim of Fiore. Like Abelard, who died around the time Joachim was born, the Calabrian mystic was castigated (not castrated!) by his enemies for political reasons. His writings seemed to support and were certainly used by the radical Franciscans who opposed the wealth and power of the papacy. Unlike Abelard, Joachim's doctrine of the Trinity emphasized the threeness of the persons of the Godhead and did so in a way that opened his doctrine to the charge of tritheism. Perhaps no Christian trinitarian thinker has ever come so close to outright tritheism than Joachim, and yet many later theologians have defended him as orthodox. Most of Joachim's books are extant in their completeness only in Latin, although excerpts have been translated into English. His most controversial works were *Concordia Novi et Veteris Testamenti* (Concordance of the New and Old Testaments) and *Liber contra Lombardum* (Book Against Lombard). In these and other works, Joachim provided both a constructive and critical contribution to the Catholic doctrine of the Trinity as formulated in the Augustinian-Anselmian tradition.

Joachim's constructive contribution to the doctrine of the Trinity lies in his historical-eschatological vision of the development of the Trinity through history. World history can be divided into three epochs in which the three persons of the Trinity are uniquely active and involved. The Father, according to Joachim, was especially active in the state of world history that began with creation and reached its conclusion with the coming of Christ. Thus, the law was given by the Father and the first person of the Trinity was the divine person most revealed and active in the era described in the Old Testament. The Son dominated the epoch of the gospel that began with the New Testament. Jesus Christ is the divine person especially revealed and active in this middle era of history. Finally, according to

Joachim, the future epoch of spiritualization of the creation itself in which God and the world will be fully united is the era of the Holy Spirit, which is dawning now but only fully realized in the future. The linkage of certain persons of the Trinity with specific epochs of world history could be consistent with the doctrine of divine attributions or appropriations, but Joachim seemed to mean something more. In his vision of God's involvement with history the persons of the Trinity are separated and affected by what they accomplish in the world.

Joachim might have been safe from the Inquisition and from condemnation by a church council had he not speculated about the necessity of the separateness of the three persons of God for history and had he not openly attacked what he perceived to be the Sabellianism of the Catholic-Orthodox doctrine of the Trinity, especially as expressed in the all-important medieval book *Sentences* of Peter Lombard. Joachim insisted that both the incarnation of the Son in Jesus Christ and the communication of the Holy Spirit to the world require "substantial distinctions" of the persons of the Trinity such that they must be conceived as "three particular, individual substances" and not merely three relations differing only in origin. Joachim argued that in the traditional doctrine as expressed by Lombard faithfully with the Augustinian-Anselmian model the three persons are reduced to mere names of God. He argued that insofar as the three persons are subordinated to the one essence of God in the classical Latin version of the doctrine of the Trinity there must be *four somethings* in God (substance and three persons) *or* only *one something* in God (substance).

To be sure, Joachim's vision of the historical triunity of God went far beyond the social analogy implied by Richard of St. Victor or any other Catholic-Orthodox Christian thinker East or West. The Catholic Church was not grateful for Joachim's critique of its standard formulations of trinitarian doctrine and condemned him and his writings at the Fourth Lateran Council (Lateran IV) in 1215. That council, considered the twelfth ecumenical council by the Catholic Church of Rome, marks a milestone in trinitarian dogma in the West due to its detailed, precise dogmatic formulation. Against Joachim and in concert with Peter Lombard (1095-1169) (who stood in the Augustinian-Anselmian tradition of trinitarian reflection) the council affirmed as dogma that the one divine substance or essence is absolutely simple (unified in every way) and never changing (unaffected by history) and that the three persons of Father, Son, and Holy Spirit are nothing more than distinct relations within the divine substance distinguished only by their differing relations of origin with regard to one another. The Father is identical with the divine nature but not with the Son who is also identical with the divine nature but not with the Father by whom he is eternally generated (begotten). The Holy Spirit is identical with the divine nature but not with the Father or the Son from whom he proceeds equally and eternally *(filioque)*. The three persons are truly three, but not "three others." Some modern critics have argued that the Lateran IV council in effect dogmatized an unfortunate distinction between *de Deo uno* (oneness of God) and *de Deo trino* (threeness of God), placing a strong priority on the former to the detriment of the latter.[9] Ever since then (and possibly before as well) the Catholic-Orthodox doctrine of the Trinity, especially in the West, has been plagued by a tendency to begin with and emphasize the unity of the Trinity in the divine substance and neglect the Trinity as community of distinct divine persons perfectly unified in love.

Thomas Aquinas represents the pinnacle of medieval scholastic and speculative theology. His grand synthesis of revelation and reason and systematic vision of all Christian philosophy and theology as expressed in massive multi-volume sets such as *Summa theologiae* (or *Summa theologica*) are usually considered almost synonymous with scholastic theology and with normative Catholic thought. He has been declared "The Angelic Doctor of the Church" by popes and his theology baptized as normative for all Catholic thought by councils. During his own lifetime (1224-1274), spent mostly in Paris teaching and writing theology at the university there, the Italian-born Dominican friar was controversial due to his attempt to integrate the newly discovered Aristotelian metaphysics and logic with divine revelation and Christian tradition. His theology attempted to discover and express the proper relationships between "nature and grace" (e.g., natural reason and faith) and between the mystical-spiritual traditions of Christian thought and the rational-logical approaches of scholasticism. The philosophies of Plato and Aristotle both found expression in Aquinas's system of theology, as did the seemingly competing trinitarian visions of Anselm and Richard of St. Victor. Thomas Aquinas was a theological genius for many reasons, not the least of which was his ability to bridge seemingly unbridgeable chasms and combine seemingly incompatible approaches.

---

9. See Karl Rahner, *The Trinity*, trans. Joseph Donceel (New York: Seabury Press, 1974), pp. 15-21.

A complete account of Thomas Aquinas's trinitarian contribution would consume much more space than is permitted here. Suffice it to say (and to then briefly explain) that it centered around his subtle, creative synthesis of the traditional Augustinian psychological model and the communal-social model of Richard of St. Victor. Almost without doubt, Aquinas's version of the unity and multiplicity of the triune being of God is closest to the Augustinian-Anselmian version, but he tried to do justice to the Victorine version as well. For Aquinas, the unifying divine nature (God's substance) is a rational-intellectual essence, that is, an eternal mind without temporal, discursive thought. A "person" is a "distinct subsistent in [or of] an intellectual nature."[10] An intellectual nature requires some degree of multiplicity, as does love — which God is, as well as intellect. The intellectual love of the Father gives rise to the eternal begetting of the Son who is distinct from the Father only in being generated (begotten) by him from all eternity. The love between the Father and Son gives rise to the eternal procession of the Holy Spirit from both of them as their "bond of love" which is distinct from them only in proceeding forth from them eternally.

Questions still remain about Aquinas's vision of the triunity of God. Are these three relations (Father, Son, Holy Spirit) truly "persons" in the full sense or would a better term for them be "modes of being" or "subsistences of the substance"? Karl Rahner, a leading twentieth-century Catholic trinitarian theologian, has argued that "mode of being" is a better term than "person" for naming the multiplicity within the Trinity, because no matter how one tries to avoid it "person" inevitably means to most people "a distinct center of consciousness and will."[11] And yet, Thomas Aquinas clearly did not wish to reduce the multiplicity within the divine being to mere names or modes of being. Second, did Aquinas really take a step beyond the Augustinian-Anselmian emphasis on the unity of the divine being or did he also contribute to the *operational modalism* that plagues so much Western Christian thought? By placing consideration of the divine unity of nature *(de Deo uno)* first and foremost and then attempting to find "room" for the multiplicity of persons *(de Deo trino)* and especially by identifying the divine unity with the spiritual-intellectual nature of God, Aquinas *seemed* to deepen the problems of trinitarian theology in the West.

10. Fortman, *The Triune God*, p. 208.
11. Rahner, *The Trinity*, pp. 103-15.

The Councils of Lyons and Florence are generally considered the two "reunion councils" because they included delegates from both the Greek Eastern and Latin Western halves of Christendom and promulgated dogmatic assertions that were intended to achieve unity of East and West by overcoming the unfortunate divisions caused by the *filioque* clause in the Western creed. The Second Council of Lyons met in 1274 in Lyons, France, and was attended by the Patriarch of Constantinople and two representatives of the Byzantine emperor. Pope Gregory X called the council and presided over it. The dogmatic significance of the council consists in the "Constitution on the Procession of the Holy Spirit," which received support from both the Eastern delegates and the Western bishops and thus achieved formal reunion of the Greek and Latin churches. It affirms the *filioque* clause and concept as well as the concept that the Holy Spirit proceeds from the Father and the Son "not as from two principles but as from one, not by two spirations [processions] but by one." The latter qualification seems to have satisfied the Eastern delegates, who objected to the *filioque* clause on the basis that it involves a "double procession" of the Spirit that creates havoc for the unity of the Trinity as well as for the equality of the Spirit with the Father and the Son.

Lyons II promulgated the following very succinct and relatively clear dogma of the Trinity:

We believe in the Holy Trinity, Father, Son and Holy Spirit, one omnipotent God and deity entire in the Trinity; co-essential, consubstantial, co-eternal and co-omnipotent, of one will, power, and majesty, the creator of all creatures. . . . We believe that each single person in the Trinity is the one true God complete and perfect. . . . We believe in the Son of God, the Word of God, eternally born of the Father, consubstantial, co-omnipotent and entirely equal to the Father in divinity. . . . And we believe in the Holy Spirit, complete, perfect, and true God, proceeding from the Father and from the Son, co-equal, consubstantial, co-omnipotent and co-eternal with the Father and the Son in all things. We believe that this Trinity is not three gods but one God, omnipotent, eternal, invisible and unchanging.[12]

12. From Fortman, *The Triune God,* p. 218.

The Council of Florence (1438-1445) was the last general or ecumenical council of the Latin church to concern itself with dogmatic formulation of the doctrine of the Trinity. It repeated much of what was already stated by Lyons II, with Greek delegates once again in attendance and agreeing to language that included *filioque* qualified by the assertion that the Holy Spirit proceeds from both Father and Son as from one principle (not two) and in one procession (not two). Florence also dogmatized Anselm's famous trinitarian concept that "in God everything is one where opposition of relation [i.e., origination] does not intervene." While the intention was to protect the unity of the divine essence against the threat of tritheism, this principle may be interpreted modalistically as reducing the divine persons to modes of being of the one divine intellectual substance. Due to both geopolitical and theological exigencies, however, the reunion of East and West achieved by both the Councils of Lyons and Florence dissolved later. Nevertheless, the doctrines of the Trinity promulgated by these councils laid the foundation for future dialogues and agreements and eventual possible reunion of the two halves of Christendom (as they recognize one another).

In general, the medieval era of theology in the West was a time of tidying up trinitarian doctrine within the Catholic-Orthodox tradition stemming from the early church fathers and especially Augustine. That is, few major leaps in creative thinking about the Trinity were achieved and those that were attempted, such as Joachim of Fiore's, were condemned as heretical. Much energy was focused and expended on scholastic projects of proving trinitarian dogma logically necessary or at least consistent with logic. The emphasis of most Latin thinkers was on the unity of the divine substance conceived intellectually (i.e., as mind and thought) and with a few exceptions (such as Richard of St. Victor's theology) the distinctness of the persons was compromised by being reduced to relations.

At the end of the medieval era and on the cusp of the great reformations of the sixteenth century, Renaissance humanist Christian thinkers of Europe like Erasmus of Rotterdam (1466-1536) were fed up with what they perceived to be the over-fussiness and hairsplitting arguments of the scholastic theology of the middle ages. Erasmus' "Philosophy of Christ"[13]

13. For the main outlines of Erasmus's "Philosophy of Christ" see his *The Handbook of the Militant Christian (Enchiridion)* in John P. Dolan, ed., *The Essential Erasmus* (New York: Mentor-Omega Books, 1964).

was offered as a simple (if not simplistic) alternative to "theology" that revolved entirely around striving to emulate the character of Christ in all human relations through prayer and knowledge. Erasmus and other Renaissance humanist reformers of the church eschewed speculative constructions of trinitarian doctrine in preference for "following Christ." Out of sheer disgust for the extremes of medieval scholasticism these Christian humanists seemed about to cast away all theological reflection. It was into that milieu that Martin Luther and the other Protestant reformers stepped, and it is to the stories of their theological reflections on the Trinity that we now turn.

The Reformers' Contributions
and Post-Reformation Neglect

For the most part the Protestant reformers considered the doctrine of the Trinity a settled matter and refused to reconsider its essential content as expressed in the Nicene Creed and worked out in the writings of Augustine. The fundamental affirmation of God's triunity as one being or substance and three eternal persons or subsistences was considered an essential of orthodox Christian doctrine by nearly all the Protestants. On the other hand, the leading Protestant reformers were critical with varying degrees of harshness of what they considered the overly speculative and too detailed scholastic developments of the trinitarian dogma. In reaction against medieval scholastic theology some Protestants such as Martin Bucer of Strasbourg (1491-1551) wished to move away from traditional non-biblical language about the inner-trinitarian relations of unity and distinction such as *homoousios* and possibly even "Trinity" itself. The main Protestant theologians such as Martin Luther (1483-1546), Ulrich Zwingli (1484-1531), and John Calvin (1509-1564), however, affirmed the necessity of using extra-biblical terms to protect the biblical teaching about God and defended the relative authority of the early Christian creeds about God and Christ. That is not to say that they appreciated all the medieval scholastic language and debates over the eternal divine "processions" and "relations," however. They did not. Like many of the Renaissance Christian humanists (e.g., Erasmus), Luther, Zwingli, and Calvin eschewed too much rationalistic peering into the mysteries of the inner life of the Godhead and sought as much as possible to affirm the dogma of the Trinity carved out in the patristic era while avoiding scholastic hairsplitting.

During the momentous sixteenth century some new reflection on the Trinity became unavoidable as the success of the Protestant reformation begun by Luther and Zwingli created the freedom to challenge more Christian traditions than they did. So-called "anti-trinitarian rationalists" from Spain and Italy and other parts of Europe sought refuge in Protestant territories and attempted to persuade Protestants to throw off not only traditional Catholic doctrines of salvation and sacraments but also those having to do with the person of Christ and the Trinity. The challenges of these radical reformers, such as Michael Servetus (1511-1553) and Faustus Socinus (1539-1604), forced the mainline, magisterial reformers who wished to remain orthodox in terms of Nicene faith in the Trinity to defend a continuing belief in the Trinity among their followers.

Martin Luther is usually credited with being the catalyst and main leader of the Protestant reformation of the sixteenth century. Both before and after nailing his famous "Ninety-five Theses" to the cathedral doors in Wittenberg, Germany, in 1517 he was arguing against the medieval scholastic theological tradition of emphasizing logic and speculation in doctrinal reflection and against his own followers and other Protestants who wished to discard every aspect of the church's tradition, including the Nicene Creed and the doctrine of the Trinity. Against the medieval scholastic theologians and their heirs the German reformer vehemently rejected speculation into the inner workings of the triune life of the Godhead in eternity. He labeled scholastic metaphysics a "seductress" (sometimes translated "whore") and expressed the desire that the entire science of metaphysics be "boldly crucified" in the search for God. While affirming the unity of God as one eternal, undivided, divine essence and the threeness of the persons as eternal distinctions within that one shared essence, Luther appealed to a limit of incomprehensibility within God beyond which reason must not go. "How this intertrinitarian relation is carried on is something we must believe; for even to the angels, who unceasingly behold it with delight, it is unfathomable. And all who have wanted to comprehend it have broken their necks in the effort."[14] On the

---

14. Quoted in *What Luther Says: A Practical In-Home Anthology for the Active Christian,* ed. Ewald M. Plass (St. Louis: Concordia Publishing House, 1959), p. 1385. Taken from Luther's comments on the ecumenical creeds in 1538.

other hand, against those Protestants who wished to discard the language of Trinity and possibly even the doctrine itself, Luther asserted that salvation depends on belief in it. Against all deniers of the Trinitarian faith (as expounded in the Nicene Creed) Luther declared, "This is the faith; so the faith teaches; here stands the faith. Naturally, I mean the Christian faith, which is grounded in Scripture. But he who does not want to believe Scripture but runs after reason — why, let him run. . . . This is a matter of either believing or of being lost."[15]

If Luther introduced any new element into the doctrine of the Trinity (besides rejecting over-rationalistic speculation) it would be an emphasis on the distinctness of the three persons. Luther was not afraid to emphasize that in the scriptural witness Father, Son, and Holy Spirit are "three different persons" even as they are of the same, identical divine essence. While admitting that no earthly illustration can possibly do justice to the heavenly reality of the Trinity, Luther used a "homely, simple illustration" to help people who struggled with the Trinity to understand it. "As a bodily son has flesh and blood and his being from his father, so the Son of God, begotten by the Father, has His being and nature from the Father from eternity."[16] Immediately after offering this analogy, the reformer admitted that it could not do justice to the unity of Father and Son within the eternal Godhead. However, together with other statements of the Trinity made by Luther, it illustrates his tendency to think of the three persons of God as distinct persons of love in community along the lines of Richard of St. Victor. It would be misleading to claim Luther as an example or advocate of the "social analogy" of the Trinity, but he certainly was not locked into the Augustinian psychological analogy that tended to reduce the persons of God to mere relations of origin.

Luther's protégé, right-hand man, and successor as leader of the Lutheran wing of the Protestant reformation was Philip Melanchthon (1497-1560), who provided a more systematic account of Lutheran Protestantism than Luther did. Melanchthon was influenced by both Luther and the Renaissance Christian humanists such as Erasmus. While much less harsh in his condemnations of reason than Luther was, like the latter Melanchthon

---

15. Quoted in Plass, ed., *What Luther Says*, p. 1385. Taken from Luther's 1538 comments on the creeds.

16. Quoted in Plass, ed., *What Luther Says*, p. 1386. Taken from Luther's July 7, 1537, sermon on John 1:1-2.

eschewed metaphysical speculation into the eternal inner workings of the Trinity ("immanent Trinity") in favor of an emphasis on the works of God for us in salvation history ("economic Trinity"). Nevertheless, in the Augsburg Confession,[17] for which he was largely responsible, Luther's lieutenant affirmed quite unambiguously the teaching of the decree of the Council of Nicea concerning the unity of the divine essence and concerning the three persons. Augsburg also condemned all the known heresies regarding the Trinity and labeled deniers of the Nicene faith "idolaters" and declared that they insult God and are outside the church of Christ.

Melanchthon's *Loci Communes* was written in 1555 and constitutes the earliest Lutheran systematic theology. In it Luther's heir as theological leader of the Lutheran wing of the reformation supported the traditional doctrine of the Trinity but rejected detailed metaphysical speculations about the intertrinitarian relations of origin, generation, and procession. Melanchthon went beyond anything found in Luther in defining terms like "person" in his treatment of the Trinity, but drew back from scholastic logical precision in describing the orthodox doctrine. He defined "person" in the Trinity as "an essence, a living thing in itself, not the sum of many parts but a unified and rational thing which is not sustained and supported by any other being as if it were but an addition to it."[18] Like Luther, Melanchthon emphasized the distinctness of the three persons within the history of salvation so that each person has his own distinctive work. The Son, for example, is uniquely "mediator, redeemer, and savior" and the Spirit is the one who strengthens Christians in heartfelt joy and love toward God. Beyond these distinct offices and functions Melanchthon was reluctant to speculate except to say that within the Godhead they are perfectly unified in essence and power *and* the Son is eternally begotten of the Father and the Spirit proceeds from the Father and the Son *(filioque)* and is the love and joy between them. Thus, Melanchthon brings the Lutheran doctrine of the Trinity firmly within the general Augustinian-Anselmian tradition while at the same time emphasizing the distinct functions of the three persons. Ever since Luther and Melanchthon the Lutheran tradition of trinitarian thought has emphasized the *mystery* and even the *paradox* of

17. For the entire Augsburg Confession see John H. Leith, ed., *Creeds of the Churches: A Reader in Christian Doctrine from the Bible to the Present* (revised edition) (Richmond, Va.: John Knox Press, 1973), pp. 63-107.

18. *Melanchthon on Christian Doctrine: Loci Communes 1555,* trans. and ed. Clyde Manschreck (New York: Oxford University Press, 1965), p. 11.

the divine triunity and eschewed over-rationalizing accounts of the eternal, immanent trinitarian being while insisting that affirmation of God's perfect unity of essence and distinctness of three persons is essential to true gospel faith and Christian orthodoxy.

Ulrich Zwingli and John Calvin were the two major founders and leaders of the early Reformed branch of the Protestant reformation. Zwingli was the catalyst of the Swiss reformation and arrived at many of the same ideas as Luther around the same time that the German reformer was working in Saxony. Calvin was the reformer of the French-speaking Swiss city of Geneva. He was the great systematizer of Reformed theology and was deeply influenced by Luther and Zwingli, but was much more inclined toward reasonable explication of Protestant thought than either of the two older reformers. Like them and like Melanchthon, Calvin eschewed scholastic rationalism and metaphysical speculation, but he was concerned to draw together all the loose strands of Protestant theology into a coherent, systematic account without imposing on it an alien philosophical framework.

Calvin's main trinitarian reflections appear in his mature edition (1559) of his great system of Reformed theology *Institutes of the Christian Religion* and especially in book I, chapter XIII, "In Scripture, From the Creation Onward, We Are Taught One Essence of God, Which Contains Three Persons." There the Genevan reformer uses Scripture, reason, and tradition (church fathers) to refute the anti-trinitarian Protestants such as Michael Servetus. Calvin quotes Gregory of Nazianzus approvingly and suggests that Augustine's *De Trinitate* provides all that is really needed by way of orthodox reflection on the Trinity. Calvin criticizes both deniers of the Trinity — accusing them of being responsible for nearly all heresies — and metaphysical speculators who are not content with the simple faith of the New Testament and early church but wander into vain, "evanescent speculation" by trying too subtly to penetrate into sublime mystery. Calvin sums up "the measure of faith" in the Trinity thus:

> When we profess to believe in one God, under the name of God is understood a single, simple essence, in which we comprehend three persons, or hypostases. Therefore, whenever the name of God is mentioned without particularization, there are designated no less the Son and the Spirit than the Father; but where the Son is joined to the Father, then the relation of the two enters in; and so we dis-

tinguish among the persons. But because the peculiar qualities in the persons carry an order within them, e.g., in the Father is the beginning and the source, so often as mention is made of the Father and the Son together, or the Spirit, the name of *God* is peculiarly applied to the Father. In this way, unity of essence is retained, and a reasoned order is kept, which yet takes nothing away from the deity of the Son [or] the Spirit.[19]

Calvin believed that attacks on the Nicene doctrine of the Trinity by anti-trinitarians as well as by Jews and Moslems and skeptics undermined the gospel itself. He was not at all interested in the doctrine of the Trinity for speculative reasons or in order merely to support the authority of tradition. For him, the trinitarian confession (as stated briefly above) is necessary in order to express and protect belief in salvation and Jesus Christ. Any diminution of the full Nicene trinitarian faith (not necessarily the whole product of post-Nicene trinitarian tradition) is necessarily an attack on Jesus Christ as redeemer, the Holy Spirit as sanctifying power, and salvation as a work of grace wrought entirely by God. Calvin's exact formulations of the doctrine of the Trinity are often influenced by and reminiscent of Augustine, but like Luther his main concern is with the Trinity as the biblical expression of "God for us" in creation, redemption, and sanctifying renewal. Like Luther also, Calvin tends to emphasize the distinctiveness of the three persons or "subsistences" while continually affirming their unity as one God in an eternal and indissoluble single essence.

The radical wing of the Protestant reformation included a wide variety of reformers and their followers who for various reasons and in diverse ways rejected much more of the tradition than did Luther, Zwingli, or Calvin. Among the reformation radicals were the Anabaptists such as Balthasar Hubmaier (d. 1528) and Menno Simons (d. 1561) as well as the rationalistic anti-trinitarians Michael Servetus and Faustus Socinus. It is dangerous to lump these reformers together into a single category because they had little or nothing in common other than being on the persecuted fringes of the Protestant reformation for variously rejecting much more of the traditions of Christendom than the so-called "magisterial reformers" such as Luther, Zwingli, and Calvin. Among the traditions of Christendom rejected by al-

19. John Calvin, *Institutes of the Christian Religion,* I, XIII, 20, ed. John T. McNeill, trans. Ford Lewis Battles (Philadelphia: Westminster Press, 1960), p. 144.

most all of the radical reformers were the existence of state-supported churches, infant baptism, and high liturgical styles of worship. They tended to take the Protestant principle of *sola scriptura* much further than Luther, Zwingli, Calvin, or the English reformers ever intended. This led them to criticize the magisterial reformers for relying on formal creeds, confessions of faith, and the magisterial decisions of past councils as well as highly refined theological arguments rather than resting their doctrinal affirmations solely on Scripture alone. The anti-trinitarians wished to retain biblical language about Father, Son, and Holy Spirit while discarding completely the entire tradition of Nicene orthodoxy in both its form and content. The Anabaptists, on the other hand, by and large remained operationally Nicene while demoting trinitarian language to second-order status insofar as it was not strictly biblical language.

The Anabaptist leaders and thinkers such as Hubmaier and Menno Simons believed strongly in the triunity of God while reducing it to a bare biblical minimum. Without openly criticizing or rejecting Nicene orthodoxy or the church's developed trinitarian dogma, these radical reformers neglected any precise explication of the unity of the three divine persons or of their distinctness within an eternal order of relations. All of that early and medieval doctrinal development they regarded as wasted effort in comparison with the much more important tasks of evangelism and discipleship. Their theological writings tended to focus on those matters where they differed from the magisterial reformers — especially the proper recipients and forms of baptism. All of the Anabaptists believed in and practiced believer baptism by pouring or effusion. More important than the precisely correct forms of baptism, however, was the experience baptism figures and proclaims — regeneration by the Spirit of God. Typical of Anabaptist statements is Hubmaier's frequent declaration against baptismal regeneration (salvation by baptism of infants): "we must be born again or we cannot see the kingdom of God, nor enter it."[20] Nevertheless, against the anti-trinitarians who sometimes made inroads into Anabaptist circles, Menno Simons produced a tract or brief treatise in defense of the biblical teaching about the Trinity entitled *Confession of the Triune God* (1550). In true Anabaptist fashion he intended and attempted to stick

20. Balthasar Hubmaier, "On the Christian Baptism of Believers," in *Balthasar Hubmaier: Theologian of Anabaptism*, ed. and trans. H. Wayne Pipkin and John H. Yoder (Scottdale, Penn.: Herald Press, 1989), pp. 95-149.

strictly to biblical language and avoid use of "human sophistry and glosses" (i.e., extra-biblical, metaphysical language). He appealed not at all to any creeds or conciliar decisions, including those of Nicea and Constantinople. According to Menno, "to go beyond the simple language of the Bible in matters like this [viz., explaining the Trinity] was 'like trying to pour the river Rhine . . . into a quart bottle.'"[21]

The core of Menno Simons's statement of belief in the Trinity is this:

> Dear brethren in the Lord, we believe and confess that this same eternal, wise, almighty, holy, true, living, and incomprehensible Word, Christ Jesus, which was in the beginning with God and which was God, incomprehensible — born of the incomprehensible Father, before every creature — did in the fullness of time become, according to the unchangeable purpose and faithful promise of the Father, a true, visible, suffering, hungry, thirsty, and mortal man in Mary, the pure virgin, through the operation and overshadowing of the Holy Spirit, and so was born of her.[22]

To be sure, there is nothing here that even remotely reminds of the highly subtle, semi-philosophical language of the Great Tradition about the Trinity developed over fifteen hundred years prior to Menno's writing. In other places in his *Confession* he does briefly dip into that language to expand on the core of his belief in the Trinity. He affirms, for example, that the Holy Spirit "proceeds from the Father through the Son, although he ever remains with God and in God." Thus, even Menno Simons, in spite of every intention to "speak where Scripture speaks and remain silent where Scripture remains silent," could not avoid borrowing at least minimally from the Great Tradition of trinitarian doctrinal formulation and reflection outside of biblical language itself. Clearly, Menno Simons and the other major Anabaptist leaders were at least operationally orthodox in terms of their belief in the Trinity, and their followers in the various branches and offshoots of the Anabaptist movement (Mennonites, River Brethren, Churches of the Brethren, etc.) have remained so for four and a

21. Quoted in Timothy George, *Theology of the Reformers* (Nashville: Broadman Press, 1988), p. 275.
22. Quoted in Walter Klaassen, *Anabaptism in Outline: Selected Primary Sources* (Scottdale, Penn.: Herald Press, 1981), p. 39.

half centuries without officially endorsing or requiring confession of trinitarian creeds.

The other major branch of the radical reformation was constituted by a relatively diverse group of unorthodox Protestants — rejected from Protestantism by other Protestants — known as the anti-trinitarians or anti-Nicenes. The two best-known such heretics of the Protestant reformation during the sixteenth century were those already mentioned: Michael Servetus and Faustus Socinus. These and others like them went even further than Anabaptists like Menno Simons and Balthasar Hubmaier in rejecting doctrinal traditions and insisting that all beliefs retained within Protestantism must be in strict accordance with both Scripture and reason and that this principle required rejection of the classical, orthodox doctrine of the Trinity. Their doctrinal reflections harked back to the non-trinitarians of the third century such as Arius and his followers and foreshadowed (and perhaps influenced indirectly) the rise of Unitarianism in the late eighteenth and early nineteenth centuries. They were radical monotheists with a Christocentric emphasis. That is, they believed that once one stripped away all of the traditional accretions of trinitarian speculation the simple biblical message of Jesus Christ as a prophet of God and the Holy Spirit as another name for God's presence in the world could be found.

Many historians of Christian thought regard Michael Servetus as the paradigm or prototype of a heretic of the Protestant reformation. One modern author entitled his book about the Spanish doctor and theologian *Michael Servetus: A Case Study in Total Heresy*.[23] Throughout the fourth and fifth decades of the sixteenth century Servetus traveled around the Protestant cities of Europe attempting to engage leading Reformed theologians in debates about the Trinity, which he believed, in its classical formulations at least, to be a corruption of the biblical witness and contrary to reason. He also published two major works against the dogma entitled *Concerning the Errors of the Trinity* (1531) and *Dialogues on the Trinity* (1532). Like many theological reformers, Servetus wished to provide a magnum opus or great work summing up his proposals for theologically sound change in the beliefs and practices of Christendom. In 1553 he secretly and anonymously published *The Restoration of Christianity*, which

---

23. Jerome Friedman, *Michael Servetus: A Case Study in Total Heresy* (Geneva: Librairie Droz S.A., 1978).

directly contributed to his condemnation by the Inquisition of the Catholic Church and burning at the stake by the Genevan city council under Calvin. Servetus also published several books on anatomy, medicine, and astronomy-astrology.

Although he was born in Spain, Servetus spent most of his life as a peripatetic student, teacher, lecturer, and secret writer of tracts and books on theology and true reformation. Without any doubt or debate he was one of the most brilliant and eccentric men of his time. According to one modern translator and commentator, Servetus' influence was so great around Europe that he gave both Calvin and Melanchthon serious concern for the future of the Protestant reformation's trinitarian orthodoxy. "It is this fact that gives Servetus his significance in the history of religious thought in Europe: that he was the fountain-head of the antitrinitarian tendencies that in a half-century after his time had become developed into a well-defined movement. They all seem historically to derive more or less directly from him."[24] Modern Unitarianism, which began as a distinct, organized movement in Britain and the United States in the late eighteenth century, regards Servetus as its distant founder and a truer reformer than Luther, Zwingli, or Calvin. Servetus tried on several occasions to get Calvin to hold a public debate with him on the dogma of the Trinity and specifically about whether it is biblical and reasonable. Calvin corresponded with the radical reformer and cautioned him very harshly and in no uncertain terms to stay away from Geneva. For reasons unknown Servetus showed up in church to hear Calvin preach on Sunday, August 13, 1553. He was recognized and arrested and, after a trial conducted by the city council, burned at the stake on the outskirts of Geneva. Although Calvin attempted to persuade the council to change the method of execution to beheading, he was without doubt instrumental in the unfortunate Spaniard's demise for holding unorthodox beliefs. All of Europe was divided over Geneva's treatment of a radical dissenter. The leading magisterial reformers of Germany and Switzerland — including Melanchthon — congratulated Calvin and Geneva for ridding the Protestant cause of a nuisance. Christian humanists and other radical reformers, on the other hand, raised an outcry against Calvin and the city of Geneva. Soon after Servetus' death Calvin published a kind of *apologia* for the persecution entitled *Defense of the Or-*

24. Earl Morse Wilbur, Introduction, *The Two Treatises of Servetus on the Trinity* (Harvard Theological Studies, extra number, 1932), p. xviii.

thodox Doctrine of the Trinity Against the Errors of Michael Servetus. Whether Calvin truly understood Servetus' views on the Trinity and other subjects has been much debated, as has the effect his treatment of Servetus and other dissenters and heretics should have on his overall reputation in the history of Christian theology.

If Calvin did not fully understand Servetus' doctrine of the Trinity he can hardly be blamed for that. It evolved throughout Servetus' lifetime and was very complex if not entirely inconsistent. While sometimes labeled an anti-trinitarian, Servetus was actually only anti-Nicene. That is, he "did not propose to reject the doctrine of the Trinity but rather to correct the errors of the scholastic and Nicene formulations. He would replace the philosophical argument undergirding the Trinity, which identified the substance of the three Persons (consubstantiality) with the more primitive, Biblically defensible argument of the unity of rule (the monarchianism of the Father and the Son and the Holy Spirit."[25] His formulation of the doctrine of the Trinity was an odd combination of Sabellianism (modalism) and subordinationism (either Arianism or adoptionism). He was accused of both, but primarily convicted and burned for the latter. He refused to acknowledge a strict identity of being between the person of Jesus Christ and the eternal, divine Word of God whom he considered one of the "wonderful dispositions of God" in which God's divinity shines forth. Jesus Christ, according to Servetus, was the Son of God but not God the Word except in manifestation (revelation). The Holy Spirit is not a distinct being or third person emanating from the Father or the Word but "an activity of God himself" in creation and redemption.

Faustus Socinus (or Fausto Sozzini) was more clearly non-trinitarian or anti-trinitarian than Servetus, but influenced at least indirectly by him. Unlike the Spanish doctor-theologian, however, Socinus helped found and led a radical reformation movement that evolved into a denomination: the Minor Reformed Church of Poland. The latter may have been the first organized expression of Unitarianism, although in the sixteenth and seventeenth centuries it was considered Anabaptist. Faustus Socinus' uncle Lelio Socinus (1525-1562) was an influential Italian lawyer, humanist, and convert to radical Protestantism who traveled around Europe meeting and corresponding with various reformers, including Calvin. Lelio Socinus

---

25. George H. Williams, *The Radical Reformation* (Philadelphia: Westminster Press, 1962), p. 322.

gradually adopted and defended anti-Nicene, if not anti-trinitarian, views of the Godhead. His rejection of the orthodox doctrine of the Trinity was sparked in part, at least, by his interest in the reasons for Servetus' execution in Geneva. He was living in Switzerland when the Spanish radical reformer was burned at the stake and expressed such horror that Heinrich Bullinger, Zwingli's successor as chief pastor of Zurich, required the Italian to denounce Servetus' heresies and write a confession of faith in the Trinity. Socinus complied in *Confessio de Deo* (1555) but proceeded later to publish anti-Nicene works such as *Theses de Filio Dei et Trinitate* (1560).

Faustus Socinus visited his uncle Lelio in Zurich, and when the latter died in 1562 his nephew gathered up his library and moved to Poland where for a few decades there existed a relative official toleration of radical religious ideas. Before reaching Poland, the younger Socinus wrote at least two books in which he denied Christ's essential deity and the multiplicity of persons within the Godhead, books that have never been translated wholly into English: *De Explicatio* (a treatise on the prologue to John's gospel) (1562) and *De Jesu Christo Servatore* (1578). After arriving in Poland in 1580 Faustus Socinus applied for membership in an Anabaptist sect known as the Polish Brethren or Minor Church. After a period of examination during which he was required to explain his views on a variety of controversial issues dear to Anabaptists, the Italian transient and radical reformer was admitted to the church and gradually came to dominate it theologically. Shortly after his death in 1604 his followers wrote and published the famous *Racovian Catechism*, which was heavily influenced by Faustus Socinus and probably represents the first Unitarian creed. For a few decades in the late sixteenth and early seventeenth centuries the Polish Minor Church/Polish Brethren thrived in and around the city of Rakow with its own seminary and publishing house. Eventually, the Polish government suppressed it, and many of the Socinians (as they came to be known) went into exile in Holland and England. While there is no direct connection organizationally between them and the first Unitarian churches and societies in the late eighteenth century in London, their earlier presence made that later development possible.

Like Servetus, Socinus rejected the Nicene Creed and Nicene dogma of the Trinity on two grounds — Scripture and reason. He believed and argued that the orthodox distinction between "substance" and "person" in God is artificial and illogical and led the classical doctrine into all kinds of absurdities as manifested in the scholastic speculations about it in the medieval era. Socinus believed that the magisterial Protestant reformers and the leading Anabaptists such as Menno Simons had failed sufficiently to critique the traditional church and its theology and thus the reformation remained incomplete. According to him and his followers, God is perfectly one in person as well as substance or essence even though he manifests himself in various ways and under different names (Sabellianism, modalism). Socinus' radically monotheistic deity was also conceived as temporal and limited (or self-limiting) in knowledge and power. Jesus Christ, Socinus argued, was a man in whom the manifestation of God's will or Word appeared in a unique manner and who was exalted by God to a special status of power and government by the resurrection and ascension (adoptionism). He argued that Jesus Christ was *"vere deus"* (truly God) but only because the Father shared power with him at his ascension. Like Servetus he considered the Holy Spirit God's activity in the world and not a third, distinct person *(hypostasis)* in the Godhead.

By and large the main branches of the Protestant reformation (e.g., Lutheran, Reformed, Anglican, Anabaptist) rejected non-trinitarianism including anti-Nicene theology such as was developed by radical reformers like Servetus and Socinus. Socinus' theology (and through it certain aspects of Servetus') survived "underground" mainly in England until the so-called "Age of Enlightenment" in the late eighteenth and early nineteenth centuries, when laws against heresy were set aside and Unitarianism could organize as a distinct group of churches. The Lutheran confessional statements (Augsburg Confession, *Book of Concord*, etc.) strongly affirmed a required orthodoxy: the Nicene doctrine of the Trinity including the *filioque* clause. So did the Reformed confessional statements and the Church of England's *39 Articles of Religion*. The Anabaptists tended to neglect or reject highly formalized, detailed doctrinal statements, but the main Anabaptist groups such as Mennonites, Church of the Brethren, and Hutterites have always been operationally trinitarian while showing no interest whatsoever in debating or defending the fine points of the doctrine of the Trinity or repeating the Nicene Creed, either with or without the *filioque* clause.

The Roman Catholic Church added little or nothing to the medieval developments of the trinitarian dogma during the reformation age. The Council of Trent (1545-1563) formed the centerpiece and culmination of the so-called Catholic Counter-Reformation and focused primarily on anathematizing Protestants and Protestant doctrines such as unconditional election and irresistible grace and on correcting certain abuses in the church's polity and practice. The third session of this nineteenth ecumenical council (as counted by Rome) affirmed the Nicene Creed (including *filioque*) as the basis of Christian faith and condemned all who reject it.

At the end of the reformation era the doctrine of the Trinity entered into a period of neglect and decline. The focus of theological attention in the West turned to issues of salvation and the "acids of modernity" (challenges of science and Enlightenment philosophies, etc.). Only occasionally did a Christian theologian or philosopher present a new objection to or defense of the doctrine of the Trinity, and rarely did that involve anything really new. Most of the objections, such as those raised by deists in the eighteenth century, were merely repetitions of those raised by Socinus or Servetus during the reformation era. Most of the defenses and the rare examples of speculative or exegetical investigations and proposals were repetitions of ones raised by early church fathers or medieval thinkers. While great strides were being made in doctrinal reflection on salvation and the church and new developments were taking place in spirituality, the doctrine of the Trinity languished from severe neglect or satisfaction with traditional formulas.

From approximately 1600 until the twentieth century the doctrine of the Trinity remained relatively untouched. Many theologians of post-reformation orthodoxy (Protestant and Catholic) treated it as a settled issue and merely explicated and defended it against sectarian and Enlightenment skeptics, most of whom had little or nothing new or innovative to say against it. Few, if any, important treatises on the Trinity were published during the era. Here and there, occasionally, a Christian theologian wrote an article, tract, or treatise dealing with the doctrine itself or with some particular aspect of God's triunity that raised a new question or hinted at a new or forgotten perspective. In this section we will focus on the major Christian thinkers who contributed to the neglect of the doctrine of the Trinity in the post-reformation era and on those who hinted at some new angle or perspective. We will neglect those who were satisfied merely to repeat or refurbish and defend the traditional dogma.

The rise of Deism or "natural religion" in Great Britain throughout the seventeenth and eighteenth centuries presented a serious challenge to the doctrine of the Trinity; it was considered by most deists to be mysterious, supra-rational if not irrational, and one of the causes of sectarian strife within culture. Many of these Enlightenment-inspired critics of traditional dogma avoided denial of the Trinity due to blasphemy laws under which heretics could be prosecuted. However, their teachings about "reasonable Christianity" could easily be read as implicit denials of the trinitarian dogma — at least as having any role to play in modern, enlightened Christianity as it accords with reason. Among the more influential deists and proponents of natural religion and "reasonable Christianity" were John Locke (1632-1704), John Toland (1670-1722), and Matthew Tindal (1656-1733).

During the same era so-called "enthusiastic religion" (Pietism and Revivalism) countered the new skeptical Christianity of Deism with an emphasis on "heart religion" and "experiencing Christ." The leading pietists and revivalists such as Philipp Jakob Spener (1635-1705), Nikolaus Ludwig Count von Zinzendorf (1700-1760), John Wesley (1703-1791), and Jonathan Edwards (1703-1758) had little to add to the orthodox formulation of the Trinity. While the deists and rationalists tended toward an implicit anti-Nicene attitude, toward completing the reformation of the church and theology, the pietists and revivalists (evangelicals) tended to accept Nicene orthodoxy as a "given" and focus on experience of God and Christ without emphasizing the Trinity. A few of them did suggest minor revisions of trinitarian faith that did not catch on even among their followers.

Finally, the era of neglect culminated in the rise of classical liberal Protestant theology. The father of modern liberal theology was Friedrich Schleiermacher (1768-1834) and its single most influential theologian was Albrecht Ritschl (1822-1889). They and their followers looked for the "essence of Christianity" apart from the dogmatic developments of the post-apostolic eras of Christianity. For a variety of reasons they tended to relegate the dogma of the Trinity to the "Hellenization of Christianity." Without blatantly denying any and all truth to it, the liberal theologians treated the Trinity as irrelevant speculation. For all practical purposes, something akin to Servetus' or Socinus' teachings about the Trinity prevailed over Nicene orthodoxy in the liberals' doctrines of God. By the dawn of the twentieth century the doctrine of the Trinity had fallen into such severe decline from either benign neglect or skepticism that it was in danger of becoming a useless relic within the museum of dusty theology tomes.

The English philosopher John Locke is often considered one of the fathers of both modern, Enlightenment philosophy and Deism. That he was not himself a deist is made clear in his defense of miracles in *A Discourse of*

Miracles (1702). However, many interpreters of modern philosophy and theology consider Locke an influence on the rise of Deism because of his booklet *The Reasonableness of Christianity* (1695), in which the English philosopher attempted to demonstrate the concordance of reason with divine revelation and vice versa. In that process Locke neglected without openly denying or rejecting what many would consider some of the more mysterious doctrines of the Christian faith. The Trinity, for example, is not defended by Locke. One can read *Reasonableness of Christianity* from beginning to end and conclude that for Locke the Trinity and the dogma of Christ's deity and humanity ("hypostatic union") are not parts of the essence of reasonable Christianity. Locke describes Jesus Christ as the Messiah and clearly means that he was the greatest of all God's prophets in that he brought a full revelation of the will of God. For Locke, as for many Enlightenment Christian thinkers, "the Christian religion does not depend on 'speculations and niceties, obscure terms and abstract notions,' but demands belief in Jesus, whose credentials are the way he fulfilled prophecies and performed miracles."[26] Perhaps unintentionally, Locke paved the way for the stridently anti-Nicene "free-thinking" movement of so-called "Christian Deism" represented by his disciples John Toland and Matthew Tindal and their disciples in the English-speaking countries. He did that by arguing that true Christianity is always consistent with true reason even when it goes beyond what reason can now demonstrate by itself. Locke saw divine revelation as an extension of reason and not at all qualitatively above or ever in conflict with reason. One cannot help but suspect that he considered the dogmas of the early church irrational or at least too suprarational to include within "reasonable Christianity."

Locke's ardent admirer and self-styled protégé John Toland took the next step beyond Locke by publishing *Christianity Not Mysterious* one year after Locke's *The Reasonableness of Christianity* appeared. Whereas Locke had wanted to rescue Christianity by demonstrating its accordance with Enlightenment rationality, Toland seems to have wanted to undermine if not subvert Christianity — at least in the sense of Christian orthodoxy. While claiming to be a true son of the Christian church (Catholic, then Anglican) Toland argued that radically redefined Christianity is nothing other than "natural religion" — what any reasonable person observing the evi-

26. I. T. Ramsey, "Editor's Synopsis," in John Locke, *The Reasonableness of Christianity*, ed. I. T. Ramsey (London: Adam & Charles Black, 1958), p. 23.

dences of the natural world can and should believe quite apart from special revelation or faith. Toland's completely non-mysterious "Christianity" does not include concepts that can be known by faith in divine revelation alone, such as the Trinity and the incarnation. In the first chapter, the deist attacked the "doctrine" of the mysteriousness of divine revelation and dogmas as "the known Refuge of some Men, when they are at a loss in explaining any Passage of the Word of God."[27] Toland then continued to criticize those conclusions of orthodox Christianity that he considered irrational (which included everything supra-rational as well), including the dogma of the Trinity, the language of which he labeled the "barbarous jargon of the Schools." Many scholars have noted profound similarities between Toland's treatment of the Trinity and the Socinians', who had entered England from Poland where they had become a persecuted and banished sect. For Toland, as for most deists afterwards, true religion — including authentic (non-mysterious, rational) Christianity — is simply rational morality. It is living a life of virtue according to reason in the service of God and humanity and has nothing whatever to do with believing in divinely revealed mysteries that transcend natural reason.

One of the most influential Christian deists was Matthew Tindal whose *Christianity as Old as the Creation* (1730) exercised profound influence on the rise of Unitarianism and free thinking among rationalist Christians in Great Britain and its colonies. Tindal, who taught at Oxford University and was a well-known and highly regarded intellectual, published his classic when he was past seventy years old. No clearer expression of the "natural religion" of Deism can be found than Tindal's statement that:

> [T]here's a law of reason, antecedent to any external revelation, that God can't dispence, either with his creatures or himself, for not observing; and that no external revelation can be true, that in the least circumstance, or minutest point, is inconsistent with it. If so, how can we affirm any one thing in revelation to be true, 'till we perceive, by that understanding, which God hath given us to discern the truth of things; whether it agrees with this immutable law, or not.[28]

27. John Toland, "Christianity Not Mysterious," in *Deism: An Anthology*, ed. Peter Gay (Princeton: D. Van Nostrand Co., Inc., 1968), p. 54.
28. Matthew Tindal, "Christianity as Old as the Creation," in *Deism*, ed. Gay, p. 119.

According to Tindal, universal reason at its best leads to the same teachings as basic Christianity and therefore the latter is "as old as the creation." Wherever and whenever people have followed the light of natural reason in matters of religion and morality they have discovered the principles that form the core of Christian teaching. These "self-evident notions" such as the existence of one all-powerful, immutable divine being and the duty of humans to live according to the "golden rule" are the tests of all claims to special revelation. Whatever is inconsistent with or supersedes them is superfluous to religion if not pernicious. This, according to Tindal, includes the classic dogmas of the orthodox Christian churches such as the Trinity. True religion consists simply of "reasonable service" to God and humanity.

Needless to say, the "rational Christianity" of the Enlightenment free thinkers left little that is truly distinctive in Christianity. In their hands it became a vague theism with Jesus Christ as a supreme, if not unsurpassable, prophet of morality. The dogma of the Trinity they disdained because of its alleged inconsistency with universal reason and due to the supposition that it has little or nothing to contribute to morality. The influence of men like Locke, Toland, and Tindal was deep and pervasive among the educated, intellectual elite of Great Britain and North America and spread to the European continent where the same kind of thinking about religion was being promoted by French and German Enlightenment thinkers such as Lessing and Voltaire. All of this contributed to a malaise of the doctrine of the Trinity — in part, at least, because the responses by orthodox defenders of Nicene trinitarian Christianity were insipid at best. They tended merely to assert the tradition of the church and its teachings without breathing new life into them. The doctrine of the Trinity languished in spite of several so-called "trinitarian controversies" that erupted in eighteenth-century Europe and England.

Simultaneous with the rise of natural religion and Deism came the advent of so-called "enthusiastic religion" in Western (especially Protestant) Christianity. In theology and ecclesiastical life in the seventeenth and eighteenth centuries, the term "enthusiasm" was an insult. It was virtually synonymous with "fanaticism" and was an aspersion cast by both rationalists and defenders of orthodoxy at pietists and revivalists who emphasized religious experience over rational morality or theological correctness. Another label often applied to those Protestants who emphasized experience of God and Christ in conversion and spiritual devotion was (and is) "evangelicals." One of the earliest and most influential of them was the German nobleman

Nikolaus Ludwig Count von Zinzendorf, who became the leader of a band of pietistic Protestants known as the Moravians. Zinzendorf was the godson of the founder of German Pietism, the Lutheran pastor and reformer Philipp Jakob Spener, and he studied at the pietist university at Halle under the great leader of Pietism, August Hermann Francke. Zinzendorf believed that the Lutheran state church of Saxony (a state of Germany) had fallen into dead orthodoxy and formalism of worship, and he was deeply impressed by the profound Jesus-centered, experiential worship and devotional life of the Moravians whom he allowed to settle on his estate. Although their commune became known as "Herrnhut" ("the Lord's Watch") and they were often known as the "Herrnhutters" or simply the "Moravians," their official name was (in Latin) "Unitas Fratrum" ("Unity of the Brethren"). Zinzendorf became their bishop and led them into the Lutheran family of churches, although they remained semi-autonomous under him. Moravian churches still exist in various countries in the early twenty-first century.

Zinzendorf was not a systematic theologian. He was a preacher and promoter of missions, but he did study theology in order to gain recognition as a minister within the state church, and he affirmed the orthodox, Nicene dogma of the Trinity while emphasizing "heart experience of Jesus" (what modern evangelical Christians call a "personal relationship with Jesus Christ") over orthodox doctrine. He had little or no use for highly abstract systems of theology or speculation about the inner life of God ("naked Deity") apart from God's benefits for humans in salvation. In many ways he resembled the mystics of the Renaissance and reformation era. Without eschewing doctrine or morality he saw authentic Christianity as revolving around personal and corporate experience of Jesus Christ and the Holy Spirit. The only real "contribution" (if it can be called that) to the doctrine of the Trinity by the early pietists was Zinzendorf's eccentric habit of referring to and praying to the Holy Spirit as "Mother" and using the feminine pronoun of the Spirit. This was controversial even among his own Moravian followers and was rejected soon after Zinzendorf's death, only to be revived in the twentieth century by certain Protestant theologians looking for a way to incorporate feminist concerns into trinitarian language and prayers.

Zinzendorf loved to refer to the Trinity as "the holy family" and the Holy Spirit as "our dear Mother." These and similar phrases appeared in several of his published sermons, which have never been wholly translated into English.[29] In response to harsh criticism of this practice, Zinzendorf published a few sermons and dialogues attempting to show that the "motherly office of the Holy Spirit" is biblical and consistent with Christian tradition, in part, at least, because it is not an attempt to assign gender to the Spirit but only to speak of the function of the Holy Spirit in nurturing Christians spiritually after giving them new birth in regeneration. Zinzendorf distanced himself from all talk about the immanent or essential Trinity and restricted himself to speech about the economic Trinity. The former he considered an unfathomable abyss totally beyond human comprehension or speech (and yet to be acknowledged). The latter he considered to be the true focus of trinitarian language in preaching, prayer, and devotional life. And yet, Zinzendorf also argued that when he referred to the Holy Spirit as the Christian's "actual and true Mother" he was not speaking "allegorically" but "essentially."[30] That is, such language — like that of God as our Father and the Son as our brother and bridegroom — is neither arbitrary nor merely subjective but "authentically Christian." By that Zinzendorf meant both faithful to Scripture and "good for the heart." He justified motherly language for the Holy Spirit on christological grounds as well. In other words, in spite of himself, the Count could not avoid making some use of systematic theology in defense of his pneumatological speculation and language. For example, if the Christian has everything that is Christ's in the "wonderful exchange" of the incarnation and by faith in him, then the Holy Spirit who "mothered Christ" in Mary's womb becomes *relationally* the Christian's mother as well. Finally, Zinzendorf appealed to Luther to silence his critics. Luther, he pointed out, wrote that "We do not want to have a sharp dispute about the essence or substance of the Holy Spirit. The right definition and revelation of the Holy Spirit is that he is our Comforter, who comforts us like a Mother comforts her child."[31] As one modern interpreter of Zinzendorf notes,

29. For example, *"Vom Mutteramte des heiligen Geistes"* preached by Zinzendorf in London on April 23, 1747, and published in Zinzendorf's *Hauptschriften* vol. 4, ed. Erich Beyreuther and Gerhard Meyer (Hildesheim: Georg Olms Verlagsbuchhandlung, 1962-1963), pp. 1-14.

30. For an excellent exposition and discussion of Zinzendorf's trinitarian and pneumatological views see Gary Steven Kinkel, *Our Dear Mother the Spirit: An Investigation of Count Zinzendorf's Theology and Praxis* (Lanham, Md.: University Press of America, 1990), esp. pp. 79-131.

31. See Kinkel, *Our Dear Mother the Spirit,* p. 107.

In short, under the influence of Luther and Francke, Zinzendorf regarded as scriptural the idea that the Holy Spirit acted in a motherly way toward Jesus. If it was scriptural to call the Holy Spirit the Mother of Jesus, the "happy exchange" also made it scriptural, and therefore authentic Christian teaching, to speak of the Holy Spirit as the Mother of Christians and of the Christian community.[32]

Of course, Zinzendorf was accused of the heresy of tritheism by his critics due to his alleged error of importing gender distinctions (if not sexual activity!) into the Godhead itself. This charge seems to ignore the Count's adamant refusal to encroach upon the inner-trinitarian life or the Godhead "in itself" apart from God's triune relations with us in history. He affirmed the Nicene Creed and the Augsburg Confession and other trinitarian symbols (confessional statements) of the early church and the reformers. He never questioned the unity of God as one eternal substance or the equality of the persons of the Trinity. He endorsed and used the idea of the "perichoresis" of the persons of the Trinity, which refers to their "coinherence" or interpenetration of each other. Zinzendorf's critics never seemed to grasp adequately that he was speaking only of the economic Trinity and the distinct offices or functions of the three persons in salvation history. The only possible element of truth in the charge of latent tritheism in Zinzendorf's trinitarian language is his implicit neglect or rejection of the classical concept of the absolute indivisibility of the persons of God in every activity *(opera trinitatis ad extra indivisa sunt)*. Clearly he preferred a social model of the Trinity over the more traditional Augustinian psychological model. He had little or nothing to say about what he considered the speculative doctrines of the inner-trinitarian relations of generation and procession, and with regard to the controversial *filioque* clause in the Nicene Creed he claimed to affirm both that and not that. In other words, he appealed to a kind of "reverent agnosticism" when it came to questions of the inner life of God.

One of the greatest "enthusiasts" of modern evangelical Protestantism was the New England preacher, philosopher, theologian, and all-around scholar Jonathan Edwards. One of the characteristics that makes Edwards particularly interesting in the history of Christian thought is his combination of erudition and spiritual enthusiasm. That is, he was a "reasonable

32. Kinkel, *Our Dear Mother the Spirit*, p. 107.

enthusiast." Edwards is best known among the untutored in church history for his sermon "Sinners in the Hands of an Angry God," which is read and used as an example of Puritan preaching style in New England in many public school courses on American history and literature. Many people with only this passing acquaintance with Edwards misinterpret the man as a raving "hellfire and brimstone preacher" with little interest in rationality or philosophy. The fact is, however, that Edwards was by far the most erudite and well-read man of his day in New England and wrote highly abstruse treatises on a variety of subjects. He was steeped in the empirical philosophy of John Locke and kept up with all the latest developments in theology, philosophy, science, and ethics. At the same time, however, he was a leader in the revival known as the Great Awakening of the 1740s and also a passionate Calvinist.

For the most part Edwards had little new to contribute to the doctrine of the Trinity. His theological writings focused on questions of human depravity, divine sovereignty, original sin, and salvation. His sermons and theological treatises are sprinkled with orthodox allusions to the Trinity. He has never been accused of being anything less or other than fully Nicene in his theology even if his Congregationalism kept him from confessionalism. In other words, he was organically and functionally Nicene even if he did not practice or require affirmation of the Creed for ordination or church membership. Very little is known about Edwards's specific views on the subtle questions of the Trinity such as *filioque* and the differences between the generation of the Word and procession of the Spirit. However, he did compose a fascinating little piece entitled "An Essay on the Trinity" whose exact date is unknown. While the essay contains nothing particularly striking by way of new insights into or amendments to the classical Augustinian doctrine of Trinity, it does represent a brilliant defense of the *rationality* of the doctrine of the Trinity at the time of the rise of anti-Nicene Deism, and it expresses the Augustinian psychological analogy of the Trinity brilliantly and lucidly.

Edwards sets forth two guiding principles of the essay. First, he cautions that its purpose is not to explain the Trinity "so as to render it no longer a mystery."[33] The Trinity, he affirms, is an unfathomable mystery. Sec-

33. Jonathan Edwards, "An Essay on the Trinity," in *Jonathan Edwards: Representative Selections,* ed. Clarence H. Faust and Thomas H. Johnson (New York: Hill and Wang, 1962), p. 381. (All quotations from and references to this essay are from this volume.)

ond, and on another hand, he affirms that "our natural reason is sufficient to tell us that there are these three in G[od], and we can think of no more." Thus, Edwards kept one foot, as it were, firmly planted in the classical Christian tradition of affirming the ultimate mysteriousness of the Trinity while firmly planting the other foot in the contemporary Enlightenment concern for rational religion. In good Augustinian-Anselmian fashion Edwards treated the divine mystery of the Trinity as something that must be revealed; it remains always beyond complete comprehension and yet is completely consistent with human reason rightly understood and used. His essay on the Trinity represents a response to those deists such as Toland who were at that time beginning to question the reasonableness of Christian dogmas such as the Trinity and were all too willing to discard them on the supposition that they conflict with true reason.

Like Augustine, Edwards argues to the Trinity from the concept of God as mind or thought. Like Richard of St. Victor, he argues to the Trinity from the concept of God as love. In the final analysis, however, Edwards's analogy is closer to Augustine's psychological one than to Richard's social one. According to Edwards, "The sum of the divine understanding and wisdom consists in his having a perfect idea of himself, he being indeed the all: the all-comprehending being, — he that is, and there is none else."[34] A perfect idea of oneself, the Puritan then argues, is necessarily one's own object and that introduces duplicity (duality) into God. The idea that God has of himself is necessarily both God himself and God's other. From the thought process of a divine mind contemplating and beholding itself Edwards draws the conclusion that "by this means the Godhead is really generated and repeated." The Son is God's idea of himself as a distinct subsistence (person), and the Holy Spirit is the mutual love and delight that the Father and Son share. Edwards pronounces the completely rational doctrine of the Trinity thus:

> And this I suppose to be that blessed Trinity that we read of in the Holy Scriptures. The Father is the deity subsisting in the prime, un-originated and most absolute manner, or the deity in its direct existence. The Son is the deity generated by God's understanding, or having an idea of himself and subsisting in that idea. The Holy Ghost is the deity subsisting in act, or the divine essence flowing out

34. Edwards, "An Essay on the Trinity," p. 376.

and breathed forth in God's infinite love to and delight in himself. And I believe the whole divine essence does truly and distinctly subsist both in the divine idea and divine love, and that each of them are properly distinct persons.[35]

Edwards argues that the threefold distinction in the one undivided being of God is something that reason alone is sufficient to tell. If God is intelligent, personal, and self-existent, then there must be three and only three distinct "real things" in God. If Edwards's argument is valid, then it undermines the claim of the free thinkers and deists that the dogma of the triunity of God is mysterious and therefore irrational and therefore not of the essence of true religion (theism). For Edwards, true theism — let alone revealed Christianity — must be trinitarian. Edwards was trying to breathe new life into the neglected and rejected doctrine of the Trinity at a crucial juncture in the history of Christian thought. Unfortunately, his essay was not widely circulated or discussed, and rumors about it gave rise to the belief in some quarters that the author was moving away from belief in the Trinity at the time of his early death from complications of a smallpox vaccination. Clearly such rumors were wholly unfounded.

The era of liberal Protestant theology began with Friedrich Schleiermacher, whose systematic theology *The Christian Faith* (1830) has been called "with the exception of Calvin's *Institutes,* the most important work covering the whole field of doctrine to which Protestant theology can point."[36] And yet, this great classic of Protestant theology relegates the doctrine of the Trinity to an appendix-like "Conclusion" in which the author suggests that the Sabellian (modalist) view of the triunity of God might better explain the New Testament statements upon which the doctrine of the Trinity is based as well as better satisfy the religious needs of the Christian community. Without any doubt, the very short shrift Schleiermacher gave to the doctrine of the Trinity and the implicit nod he gave to one of its heresies contributed to its further neglect within Protestant theology for at least the next century.

Schleiermacher was raised in a pietist home deeply influenced by the

---

35. Edwards, "An Essay on the Trinity," p. 379. (The text is slightly altered here to replace "&" with "and," etc.)

36. "Editors' Preface" in Friedrich Schleiermacher, *The Christian Faith,* ed. H. R. Mackintosh and J. S. Stewart (Philadelphia: Fortress Press, 1928), p. v.

Moravian movement. At university, however, he came under the influence of the critical philosophy of Immanuel Kant and was influenced by the liberal religious thought of the deists and free thinkers as well. During his career as a minister and scholar he rose to prominence within the Prussian state church, which was a union of Lutheran and Reformed. He helped found the University of Berlin, pastored a leading church in Berlin, published numerous books and articles on a variety of subjects philosophical and theological, and was generally considered one of the most influential men of his day. What made Schleiermacher "liberal" was his subordination of doctrinal correctness to universal human "God-consciousness" as a feeling of utter dependence upon God. Under the influence of Romanticism, he believed that Christian doctrines must always remain open to revision and reconstruction in the light of new cultural knowledge. Doctrines, so Schleiermacher argued, are always only human attempts to bring religious feelings and experiences to expression in speech. He also relativized the authority of Scripture under the coping-stone (norm) of the "religious a priori" of *Gefühl* — the universal human awareness of being utterly dependent on something infinite such as God.

Despite his revisionist approach, Schleiermacher was sufficiently concerned with Christian tradition to elevate the unity of the essence of God with Jesus Christ to primary importance within the belief of the Christian community. That is, he was very Christocentric even if his specific doctrine of the person of Jesus Christ fell short of the orthodox doctrine of the hypostatic union. In his own way Schleiermacher attempted to preserve the central Christian intuition about and commitment to the supremacy of Jesus Christ as the man uniquely united with God's own essence in his consciousness. In his discussion of the doctrine of the Trinity the German theologian argued that its true origin and value lay in equating the divine essence in Jesus Christ with the divine essence itself. However, he proceeded to raise serious questions about the elaboration of the dogma of the Trinity in church history and suggested that at some point that process overstepped the boundaries of justified religious utterances, for "the assumption of an eternal distinction in the Supreme Being is not an utterance concerning the religious consciousness, for there it could never emerge."[37] What Schleiermacher meant, apparently, is that the full-blown orthodox dogma of the Trinity — including the idea of an immanent triunity of God in eternity —

---

37. Schleiermacher, *The Christian Faith*, p. 739.

is sheer speculation unjustified by the materials of divine revelation in Scripture and in Christian God-consciousness. He argued in his "Conclusion" to *The Christian Faith* that the "main pivots" (necessary truths) of the doctrine of Jesus Christ and the church are independent of the doctrine of the Trinity (which means the latter is something less than crucial), that the orthodox doctrine of the Trinity is plagued by inner tensions and inconsistencies, and that the doctrine of the Trinity received no "fresh treatment" in the Protestant reformation and therefore may need to be transformed in the light of its very beginnings in the primitive Christian communities. For these and other reasons Schleiermacher found the doctrine of the Trinity wanting and argued that Sabellianism, at least, could function as a Christian articulation of the basic facts of Christian revelation just as well as its Nicene alternative. Schleiermacher should not be considered "anti-Nicene" in the same sense as Servetus, Socinus, or the deists. However, he did suggest that the budding Unitarian movement in England and North America in his own time should be recognized as "by no means lacking in the specifically Christian stamp" (of God-consciousness or true piety) merely because its adherents could not reconcile themselves to the difficulties and imperfections that cling to the doctrine of the Trinity.[38]

For those who wished to remain Christians in the state churches and in the mainline Protestant denominations of England and North America, Schleiermacher's revision and reconstruction of Christian doctrine represented permission to question classical dogmatic formulations such as the Nicene doctrine of the Trinity without joining the fringe groups that openly rejected classical Christianity. Schleiermacher's theology was decidedly Christocentric in a way not true of Christian Deism, Unitarianism, or the small anti-Nicene sects that were sprouting up on the fringes of Protestantism. It appealed to many "cultured despisers of religion" (Schleiermacher's phrase for the cultural elite who valued a kind of cosmic piety but rejected orthodox dogmas) who loved Jesus Christ but hated the trappings of Christian tradition.

The second greatest theologian of liberal Protestantism was Albrecht Ritschl, whose *The Christian Doctrine of Justification and Reconciliation* (1870-1874) profoundly influenced a generation of Protestant thinkers in Europe and North America: "Not since Schleiermacher published his *Christliche Glaube (The Christian Faith)* in 1821 [first edition] has any

---

38. Schleiermacher, *The Christian Faith*, p. 749.

dogmatic treatise left its mark so deeply upon theological thought in Germany and throughout the world."[39]

Ritschl was committed to the project of discovering the genuine essence of Christianity and believed that it was the Kingdom of God as taught by Jesus Christ. This was an earthly, historical, and social reality marked by reconciliation between humans and God and between people. Influenced by the philosopher Immanuel Kant and his disciple Herman Lotze, Ritschl believed that true religion consists of values and is primarily about ethical relationships. He distinguished between two kinds of assertions: "judgments of fact" and "judgments of value," and he argued that religion (including Christianity) is interested in the latter only. Therefore, since things-in-themselves (Kant's "noumena") lie beyond human reason and knowledge and because true Christianity is interested only in values (what ought to be regardless of what is), the essence of Christianity cannot lie in metaphysical speculation or dogma about God-in-Godself but only in God's benefits for humans and in human ethical life. Ritschl and his followers attempted to carry out a complete "moralizing of dogma" such that the only valuable Christian doctrines retained would be those that relate to the Kingdom of God as a social ideal within history.

For Ritschl and his followers in classical liberal Protestant theology, then, the dogma of the Trinity was of little or no value, as it could not be related directly to ethical existence and because it was inextricable from metaphysical speculation. The Christian confession of the deity of Jesus Christ, according to Ritschl, means only that he has the value of God for us. By no means did Ritschl mean by this to demote Jesus Christ in importance for Christians, but he did mean to redefine the unique function of Jesus Christ in non-metaphysical, ethical categories. Ritschl believed that Jesus Christ pre-existed in the mind of God (a metaphysical assertion in spite of himself!) and that his will and action always agreed completely with the will of God. He was the embodiment and perfect actualization in history of the ideal of God for humanity. The Kingdom of God was realized in him and through him spread into the world. By no means did this functional Christology require a Trinity, however, so Ritschl found no particular value in that dogma. While he stopped short of completely reject-

---

39. "Editors' Preface" in Albrecht Ritschl, *The Christian Doctrine of Justification and Reconciliation*, ed. and trans. H. R. Mackintosh and A. B. Macaulay (Edinburgh: T. & T. Clark, 1900), p. v.

ing the Trinity, Ritschl practiced a kind of reverent agnosticism with regard to it and clearly treated it as non-essential to authentic Christianity.

Ritschl's disciple and scholarly interpreter and popularizer Adolf von
Harnack (1851-1930) built upon his master's foundation and attempted to
demonstrate through critical historical analysis of the church's tradition of
theological development that dogmas such as the Trinity and two natures
of Christ (hypostatic union) were products of the "Hellenization of
dogma" and thus not at all of the essence of the Christian gospel. Ritschl
and Harnack greatly influenced the North American Protestant movement
known as the "social gospel," whose leading theologian was Walter
Rauschenbusch (1861-1918). Rauschenbusch's magnum opus was published a year before his death under the title *A Theology for the Social Gospel* and represented an example of the Ritschlian moralization of dogma in
that it says almost nothing about any doctrine that cannot be translated
wholly into social-ethical categories. Without blatantly denying or rejecting the classical dogmas of orthodoxy, Rauschenbusch substituted moral
and ethical expressions for their metaphysical and (to him) speculative
ones. Thus, the unique divinity of Jesus Christ is explained this way:

> So we have in Jesus a perfect religious personality, a spiritual life
> completely filled by the realization of a God who is love. All his
> mind was set on God and one with him. Consequently it was also
> absorbed in the fundamental purpose of God, the Kingdom of
> God. Like the idea of God, the conception of the Kingdom was both
> an inheritance and a creation of Jesus; he received it and trans-
> formed it in accordance with his consciousness of God. Within his
> mind the punitive and imperialistic elements were steeped out of it,
> and the elements of love and solidarity were dyed into it. The Reign
> of God came to mean the organized fellowship of humanity acting
> under the impulse of love.[40]

The social gospel theologians, like Ritschl, had little use for the dogmas of the Trinity and the two natures of Jesus Christ. Rauschenbusch
barely mentions them. They were considered impractical and thus useless
— dead wood of tradition to be left to rot. The reactionary fundamental-

---

40. Walter Rauschenbusch, *A Theology for the Social Gospel* (New York: Macmillan Co.,
1917), pp. 154-55.

ists who jumped to the defense of Protestant orthodoxy against the rising tide of liberal theology focused more on matters of the authority of Scripture and the virgin birth and premillennial return of Christ than on the Trinity. In all of this ferment around the turn of the century the Trinity doctrine languished. To raise it up to new prominence and give it new life would take a theological revolution. Just such a revolutionary appeared quite unexpectedly in the person of a Swiss pastor named Karl Barth, who inaugurated a new era in Christian theology and revived the nearly otiose doctrine of the Trinity.

Twentieth-Century Renaissance

One of the great surprises of twentieth-century theology is the revival and revitalization of trinitarian thought in Christian theology. After centuries of neglect and stagnation, the doctrine of the Trinity became not only a fresh subject of interest and constructive attention in theology but also almost an obsession. Those who wished to continue its decline and neglect became a minority and found themselves swimming against the current or torrent of articles and books pouring forth on the subject of God's triunity. Karl Barth (1886-1968) inaugurated the revival, and it was extended by the Austrian Catholic theologian Karl Rahner (1904-1984). German-American thinker Paul Tillich (1886-1965) attempted to breathe new life into the concept of God's triunity from within a generally liberal Protestant framework. British theologian Leonard Hodgson (b. 1889) revived and updated Richard of St. Victor's and the Cappadocian fathers' social analogy of the Trinity, and German theologian Jürgen Moltmann (b. 1926) developed that analogy even further. Latin American liberation theologian Leonardo Boff (b. 1938) attempted to relate the Trinity to revolutionary sociopolitical change. Eastern Orthodox theologian John Zizioulas (b. 1931) weighed in toward the tail end of the twentieth century with a landmark book linking the doctrine of the Trinity with an ontology of being-as-community. In the midst of all this trinitarian fervor a few voices spoke out against viewing God as triune in any ontological sense. British radical theologian Geoffrey Lampe (d. 1980) sought to reduce God to the idea of Spirit apart from any immanent triune being or identity. The neo-liberal school of process theology at first attempted to develop a non-trinitarian, "bi-polar" concept of God and then gradually began to attempt to discover some level of consistency between process theology and trinitarianism. A leading figure in this project was Norman Pittenger (b. 1905). In spite of voices from the liberal camps of theology, during the later decades of the twentieth century the tide turned slowly but inexorably into a tidal wave of Christian rediscovery of and new reflection on the Trinity. Perhaps no single better example of this can be cited than the moderately feminist Catholic theologian Catherine LaCugna (1952-1997), who produced a massive interpretation of the Trinity entitled *God for Us: The Trinity and Christian Life* in the last decade of the century. Many more names and books could be mentioned to illustrate the twentieth-century renaissance of trinitarian thought in Christian theology, but these must suffice for the sake of space. The annotated bibliography appended here includes most of the important ones. Even of these selected twentieth-century trinitarian thinkers only the most important ones can be discussed here in any depth and detail. The following paragraphs will summarize the main contributions to the twentieth-century renaissance of trinitarian reflection by a half dozen or so of its major representative thinkers.

Karl Barth is without doubt the most influential Christian theologian of the twentieth century. His commentary on Romans entitled *Der Römerbrief* (1919) dropped like a bombshell on the playground of the liberal Protestant theologians. Its main thesis was that God is God — something Barth believed liberal theologians had forgotten. After establishing a new emphasis on the transcendence of God, the Swiss theologian embarked on a lifelong project of reviving a theology based entirely on the Word of God (without fundamentalism), which he wrote and published under the title *Church Dogmatics* from the early 1930s to the early 1960s. The structure of the thirteen-volume systematic theology is trinitarian, and it begins with a volume of reflection on the foundation of Christian faith in God's Word and the trinitarian nature of God's Word. According to Barth, God's Word (divine revelation) has the form of *revealer, revelation,* and *revealedness.* In other words, God "reiterates" himself in his Word. If revelation is truly revelation *of God* it must be in some way God himself. Barth's view of revelation is known as "actualism," and entails that God *is what he does.* There is no "hidden God" behind God's self-disclosure in Jesus Christ, Scripture, and the proclamation of the gospel in the church (the three forms of God's Word). Rather, when God's Word appears God is there. If God's Word has the structure of revealer, revelation, and revealedness, then God must also be triune as Father, Son, and Holy Spirit.

By tying knowledge of God to revelation as God's self-disclosure and connecting revelation inextricably with Trinity, Barth stimulated a new interest in the doctrine of God's triunity. In later volumes of *Church Dogmatics* the dialectical theologian continued to develop his trinitarian reflections further. He took what some consider a "quantum leap" in Christian theology by describing the incarnation as the Son of God's journey into a far land and bringing that journey within the triune life of God. In his doctrine of reconciliation (especially in *CD* IV/1) Barth brought the immanent and economic Trinities together by positing that the Son's journey is God's own journey and that the Son's self-humiliation in birth, life, and death is an expression of God's transcendence. God is exalted in the humility of the Son. In all of this Barth was revolutionizing so-called "classical Christian theism" along trinitarian lines. For Barth, God's being is historical in the sense that the way of the Son of God within world history and the outpouring of the Holy Spirit in time and space are events in God's own life. Barth's doctrine raises many questions about God's relationship with time and history, and in typical dialectical fashion he seems to affirm contrary things. Without doubt, however, his creative explorations of the unplumbed depths of the doctrine of the Trinity helped to usher into contemporary theology a revival of interest in it.

One controversial suggestion of Barth's was his preference for *Seinsweisen* ("modes of being") for the trinitarian distinctions. According to Barth, "persons" implies too great a difference between Father, Son, and Holy Spirit to be useful. As an English word it is a poor translation of the Greek *hypostases*. Barth wished to avoid tritheism, and he had a definite preference for Augustine's psychological analogy over the social analogy of the Trinity. This together with his penchant for drawing the triunity of God out of the eventfulness of revelation itself led some critics to charge him with implicit modalism. While modalism may have been a danger in Barth's doctrine of the Trinity very early in his career, his later reflections (e.g., in *CD* IV/1) avoid it completely. "The Way of the Son of God into a Far Country" (in *CD* IV/1) makes very clear Barth's recognition of the real, ontological distinctions of Father, Son, and Holy Spirit. There can be little doubt or debate about Barth's orthodoxy and his commitment to the Nicene faith of the early church.

In Catholic theology, Karl Rahner is the counterpart to Karl Barth. He was without doubt one of the most prolific writers and most influential thinkers the Catholic Church has produced in the modern age. He was a leading presence at the Second Vatican Council (Vatican II) in the early 1960s and continued to work for change in the church's thought and life after the Council until his death in the early 1980s. His published essays and articles fill over twenty volumes of *Theological Investigations*. Many of them relate to the doctrine of the Trinity. His best-known and most influential monograph on the doctrine, however, is entitled simply *The Trinity*. It touched off an avalanche of both Catholic and Protestant treatises on the immanent and economic Trinities, and it sparked controversy over the term "persons" for the Trinitarian distinctions.

One of Rahner's most intriguing and often-quoted and examined formulas is "The economic Trinity is the immanent Trinity and the immanent Trinity is the economic Trinity."[41] This has been dubbed "Rahner's Rule" by contemporary theologians. Rahner was concerned that too much focus on the inner life of God and especially on God's unity of being ("simplicity") led the church into a neglect of the Trinity and of the intrinsic link between it and the doctrine of salvation. He wanted to make the Trinity more practical by demonstrating its connection with salvation. His goal was to forbid or discourage all speculation about the immanent Trinity that was not relevant to salvation (including Christian life). He was convinced that the only purpose of speaking of God's immanent triune being is to guard against dissolving God into history and to protect God's transcendence and the graciousness of salvation. The immanent Trinity, however, must be regarded as the "background," so to speak, of the economic Trinity, and the economic Trinity must be regarded as the outworking of the immanent Trinity. Whatever is true of the triune being of God in the economy of salvation must be seen as true of God-in-himself, and whatever is true of God-in-himself must be seen as affected by (not constituted by) the incarnation and sending of the Spirit.

Rahner was concerned that the concept "person" may not be the one best suited to express faithfully the distinctions within the trinitarian life of God. In *The Trinity* he argued that use of "person" following medieval philosopher Boethius' definition "individual substance of a rational nature" inevitably misleads people to think of the Trinity as "three individuals." According to Rahner (closely following at least one strand of Augus-

41. Rahner, *The Trinity*, p. 22.

tine's trinitarian thought), "there are not three consciousnesses [in God]; rather, one consciousness subsists in a threefold way. There is only one real consciousness in God, which is shared by Father, Son, and Spirit, by each in his own proper way."[42] Rahner was concerned to avoid what he saw as the inevitable tritheistic implications of importing a modern, Enlightenment view of "person" as "subject" into the threefoldness of the Trinity. Boethius' definition was being revived and strengthened by Enlightenment thinkers; "person" was gradually coming to mean "self" defined over against other selves and as "center of individual consciousness." In contrast to this development Rahner suggested that the distinctions of Father, Son, and Holy Spirit be described as "distinct manners of subsisting." Thus, "the one God subsists in three distinct manners of subsisting."[43] While admitting that this language is "formalistic," Rahner defended it on the grounds that it is no more so than other, more traditional terms such as "relation" and even "person." He believed that it has the advantage of not as easily insinuating the multiplication of essences and subjectivities.

Rahner's and Barth's influences on twentieth-century trinitarian reflection can hardly be overestimated. In their own ways each one criticizes Protestant and Catholic neglect of the doctrine as well as certain traditional formulations. Each also provided constructive suggestions for revisioning the triunity of God and laid the groundwork for further construction as well as for reaction. One theologian who responded both ways — constructively and critically — and provided some of the most controversial insights about the Trinity in twentieth-century theology is German Protestant Jürgen Moltmann. Moltmann endeavored to provide the most thoroughly *trinitarian* account of the Christian God possible and wove highly suggestive, sometimes speculative and almost mystical ideas about the Trinity into his entire theological body of work. Among his most creative and influential books are *The Crucified God* (1973) and *The Trinity and the Kingdom* (1981). In these and other volumes the Tübingen theologian built on Barth's dynamic concept of the triune being of God (God as act and God's being what he does among us) as well as Barth's Christocentric focus and emphasis (God as defined by Jesus Christ and especially the cross event) while heavily criticizing the Swiss master's allegedly monistic identification of God's being with his subjectivity. Moltmann built on "Rahner's Rule" of

42. Rahner, *The Trinity*, p. 107.
43. Rahner, *The Trinity*, p. 109.

identifying (or at least never separating) the immanent and economic Trinities while criticizing any and every attempt to dilute the distinction of the persons. According to him, both Barth's and Rahner's strong emphasis on the unity of God's being and consciousness leads away from their true intentions, which were to keep the Trinity firmly grounded in God's Word (Barth) and in experience of salvation (Rahner).

In *The Crucified God* Moltmann located the meaning of the Trinity within the event of the cross of Jesus Christ. Following Luther, he argued that the "theology of the cross" is the true heart of Christian theology, and this means that whatever is inconsistent with the cross must not be affirmed of God's being. God defined himself for us in Jesus Christ and especially in his death. "[T]his means that God (himself) suffered in Jesus, God himself died in Jesus for us. God is on the cross of Jesus 'for us', and through that becomes God and Father of the godless and the godforsaken."[44] In this and similar statements the author is building on Barth's emphasis on God's being in activity: *God is who he is among us in what he does.* If the cross of Christ is the salvific event and act of God, then God is defined (self-defined!) by it. According to Moltmann, this means, then, that God is triune and radically so. He has been criticized for reviving the old heresy of "patripassianism" (suffering of the Father) and of falling into tritheism because he took the cross event so seriously as an *event in the life of God.* That is, for the German theologian, somehow or other (counterintuitively, paradoxically) the very triune life of God is constituted by the cross event so that there is a "stasis" or "moment of conflict" within God because of it. The cry of dereliction by the Son (Jesus) and the Father's rejection of the sin-bearing Son and the Spirit's emanating forth from this brokenness to absorb the pain and suffering of the sin-ridden world are not mere metaphors but events in the life of God in history and therefore (by Rahner's Rule) in the life of God in eternity!

Moltmann's trinitarian theology of the cross was at least in part an attempt to deal constructively with the crucial twentieth-century question of evil and innocent suffering. Where was God when children were being executed in the holocaust? The answer is "On the cross of their suffering." He was suffering with them. God is the "crucified God" and therefore triune. God had to suffer the loss of community within himself in order to absorb

---

44. Jürgen Moltmann, *The Crucified God,* trans. R. A. Wilson and John Bowden (New York: Harper and Row, 1974), p. 192.

and heal the brokenness of community in his world. While this is not by any means a classical philosophical theodicy, it appealed to many people in the genocidal twentieth century who believed that the only justification of God's ways is if God dies with the innocents and on their behalf. For Moltmann God does this in Christ and his cross and can do it because he is triune — a real community of three distinct persons who can experience love and the pain of love between one another.

Jürgen Moltmann worked out his trinitarian reflections more fully (and some would say more coherently) in *The Trinity and the Kingdom*. There he wove together the themes of Trinity and Kingdom of God and attempted to show that God's perfect unity as God is eschatological. It stands at the end of human history as God's goal. While there is no doubt that God will reach that goal and is, in some paradoxical way, already "there" as the power of his perfect reign of love, history is the unfolding of God's own trinitarian community through stages and patterns of interactions of Father, Son, and Holy Spirit in relation to human sin, suffering, and redemption. In this trinitarian history of the Kingdom of God each person makes his own contribution and has his own "history" both in relation to the world and in relation to the other persons. For Moltmann, the Son derives his deity from the Father and the Spirit by being dependent upon them for his establishment of the Kingdom. But the Father and the Spirit derive their deity from the Son. All three persons are interdependent in the work of the Kingdom. Moltmann developed a non-hierarchical model of the Trinity against theologies that adhere to a "monarchy of the Father" and against the *filioque* clause and its associated theology of apparent subordination of the Holy Spirit to the Son. In *The Trinity and the Kingdom* the author came very close to denying the immanent Trinity altogether or at least of dissolving it into the history of the Kingdom. However, occasionally he referred to the future as the location of both the power of God and the immanent Trinity. At least from our perspective, then, if not from God's own perspective, the only Trinity *now* ("within history") is the economic Trinity. The immanent Trinity is the eschatological unity of Father, Son, and Holy Spirit when "God is all in all."

Moltmann's entire corpus of trinitarian reflections aims at one main point: to refocus trinitarian thought away from some "heavenly and eternal *ménage-à-trois*" to the world of history, struggle, sin, pain, and death. God, Moltmann says, is truly with us in all of this mess. But he can only be truly with us if he suffers and dies and he can only suffer and die *and bring about his Kingdom* if he is a community "open to the world." The triune community of Father, Son, and Holy Spirit is the unfolding economic Trinity on the way to the future with us.

Some critics accused Moltmann's theology of being a form of "process theology." That is incorrect, however; Moltmann conceived God's "becoming" as his "historicity" rather than his "evolution." For Moltmann, God's suffering is self-chosen and God is never described by him as weak or powerless. God *freely chooses* to work by the *power of love*, which is conceived in terms of the triune love of Father, Son, and Holy Spirit overflowing in love for creation. Process theology, on the other hand, views God's relationship with the world as *intrinsic* to God's own being. Without the world there is no God. For process theology, the world (universe) is God's body and God's actual life experience is determined by the events of the world.[45] Many process theologians never developed a doctrine of the Trinity and seemed to care little about that project. One exception was British process theologian Norman Pittenger, who attempted to integrate process theology with trinitarian thought in his 1977 volume *The Divine Triunity.* Unlike Moltmann, Pittenger was willing to import real ontological limitation and change into the being of God. Relying on Alfred North Whitehead's process philosophy, the British theologian affirmed that God must not be viewed as the exception to general metaphysical principles of the world process but rather as their chief exemplification. Thus, if everything experiences some form of change in relation to other things God also must experience change in relation to the world. Pittenger sought to blend this view of God as essentially related and thus limited with the biblical portrayal of God as personal and loving. According to him,

> The belief that God is triune maintains for us the wonder and glory of the divine, guarantees for us that both personality and sociality are grounded in the way things go in the world, and opens to our minds and hearts the cosmic Love which creates us, which discloses itself to us, and which through our own response (however imperfect and feeble) enriches our lives — and adds joy to the being of God himself.[46]

45. For a summary of process theology see John B. Cobb, Jr., and David Ray Griffin, *Process Theology: An Introductory Exposition* (Philadelphia: Westminster Press, 1976).

46. Norman Pittenger, *The Divine Triunity* (Philadelphia: United Church Press, 1977), pp. 117-18.

In the final analysis, however, Pittenger was unable to provide a model of the Trinity that fit with process theology while at the same time going beyond modalism. For him, God himself is best understood as the world's and our "Cosmic Lover" and heavenly Parent — like process philosopher Whitehead's "fellow sufferer who understands." God the Parent does his best to lure and persuade each and every actual occasion ("energy event") of the world process to realize his goal for it, but God cannot coerce it to do that. So, God expresses himself into the world in Jesus Christ. The divine presence in the man Jesus is labeled by Pittenger God's "Self-Expressive Word." Also, God works in the world as a persuasive presence, luring the world toward his goal of harmony and peace. This activity of God in the world is God's "Responsive Agency." Pittenger has no concept of an immanent Trinity — eschatological or otherwise. Rather, his God is one supreme and eternal entity with three modes or functions in and toward the world. Even God's "Self-Expressive Word" is not limited to Jesus Christ although it is focused in him in a special way. These three modes of God's being are not described by Pittenger as "persons" and hardly could be so described. In spite of his good intentions, Pittenger is finally unable to provide anything even approximating the classical doctrine of the Trinity within a process framework. There is a vast difference between this quasi-modalistic, process understanding of God's triunity and Moltmann's eschatological and cross-centered trinitarian model.

Much closer to Moltmann's basic trinitarian proposal was that of an earlier British theologian of the mid-century. Leonard Hodgson taught theology at Oxford for many years and influenced a generation of English-speaking Protestant theologians away from any quasi-modalistic or even psychological concepts of the Trinity and toward a rediscovery of the ancient Eastern and Victorine concept of the social Trinity. His *The Doctrine of the Trinity* was the published form of the prestigious Croall Lectures of 1942-1943, in which he sought to expound the doctrine of the Trinity in terms of "present-day thought," one aspect of which was *empiricism*. Hodgson argued that a broad empirical examination of the religious evidence of the Christian experience of God in Christ would yield a concept of God that includes a new kind of *unity*: "an internally constitutive unity" that is organic rather than mathematical. According to Hodgson,

> The doctrine of the Trinity is thus an inference to the nature of God drawn from what we believe to be the empirical evidence given by

God in His revelation of Himself in the history of this world. I have argued that this evidence, as viewed from within the fellowship of the Christian Church, requires us to believe in a God whose unity unifies three activities each of which is made known to us as a distinct Person in the full sense of that word. Each is a He, none is an it. . . . I have attempted to show that the idea of what I have called an internally constitutive unity is not repugnant to reason.[47]

Hodgson's idea of an "internally constitutive unity" draws heavily on organic sciences. This is another example of the author's attempt to interpret the doctrine of the Trinity in terms of modern thought. He wrote that "unless I have misunderstood what I have heard of the researches of physicists, we have no actual experience of any existing unity in this world of space and time which is not of the organic type."[48] As example the British theologian cited the hydrogen atom which, though once thought to be indivisible, was in his time being perceived as complex. He also cited the phenomenon of the multi-dimensional self which consists of several elements. Perhaps most revealing was his appeal to society, which could be unified with diversity and maintain diversity while being unified. Organic unity, then, according to Hodgson, is real, concrete unity as contrasted with the abstract unity of bare mathematical "oneness." It is a unity that is consistent with multiplicity. It is the unity of parts of a whole and of a whole made up of parts.

Near the end of *The Doctrine of the Trinity* Hodgson expounded some of the practical results of thinking of the unity of God (Christian monotheism) as "internally constituted" (social) rather than as bare, mathematical oneness. Prayer, for example, may only be addressed to one of the trinitarian persons if he is a real person and not merely a mode of the divine Monad. Hodgson believed and argued that part and parcel of "trinitarian religion" is prayer addressed to the appropriate person of the Trinity and a distinct relationship to each person of the blessed Trinity. If we think of God along the lines of the social analogy "We shall speak to the Spirit as to the Lord who moves and inspires us and unites us to the Son; we shall speak to the Son as to our Redeemer who has taken us to share in His Sonship, in union with whom we are united to His Father and may address

47. Hodgson, *The Doctrine of the Trinity*, pp. 140-41.
48. Hodgson, *The Doctrine of the Trinity*, p. 94.

Him as our Father."[49] The Oxford don even went so far as to testify that before climbing into the pulpit to preach he always prayed to the Holy Spirit that his mind would be especially gifted for intense concentration so that his whole being would be involved in bringing the message home to the congregation. This was surely his way of expressing what many revivalistic Christians would call "praying for the anointing" in preaching. Hodgson believed that only if the social analogy of the Trinity dominated our thinking about God could we develop the trinitarian prayer life, which leads into rich and complex relationship to the persons of God in all their individual functions and gifts. Of course, some critics suggested that Hodgson's social analogy of the Trinity bordered on the heresy of tritheism — belief in three separate gods. He rejected this as a misunderstanding, however, and insisted that such accusations did not do justice to the *unity* of "internally constituted unity" and could have the effect of making God dependent on the world, as genuine personality always needs the "other" for its realization and fulfillment. Thus, only if God is eternally and immanently triune in this rich and complex sense could the world be a free and totally gracious gift of creation out of love and in no way a necessity for God's own personal self-realization.

Three of the finest contributions to the trinitarian renaissance in contemporary theology were published in the last decade and a half of the twentieth century. Each argued a similar thesis with distinct emphases: *that the doctrine of the Trinity is essential for Christian living because it expresses not metaphysical mumbo-jumbo but "the mystery of salvation."* Each also worked with a concept of triunity *somewhat* like Hodgson's "social analogy" while appealing to "Rahner's Rule" that the immanent Trinity is the economic Trinity and vice versa. Two were written by Roman Catholics and one by a British Eastern Orthodox theologian. The Roman Catholic theologians attempted to interpret the doctrine of the Trinity in the light of liberation theology and feminist theology as well as in the light of the Great Tradition of the church's magisterial teaching. These three authors and books are: Leonardo Boff of Brazil and his volume *Trinity and Society* (1988), Catherine Mowry LaCugna of Notre Dame University and her treatise *God for Us: The Trinity and Christian Life* (1991), and John D. Zizioulas of Glasgow, Scotland, and his essay *Being As Communion: Studies in Personhood and the Church* (1985).

49. Hodgson, *The Doctrine of the Trinity,* pp. 179-80.

105

Brazilian Catholic theologian Leonardo Boff was silenced by the Vatican for a period of time due to some of his allegedly radical proposals regarding liberation theology, and his view of Mary as the unique personal expression in humanity of the Holy Spirit (if not the incarnation of the Holy Spirit). Although some of his controversial opinions are adumbrated in *Trinity and Society*, the book is not as controversial as one might expect. And yet, it weaves together in a creative way some of the major concerns and themes of late twentieth-century theology. It is written from within a two-thirds world perspective and in the context of structural poverty, with an eye toward radical social transformation in light of the values of the Kingdom of God. It attempts to breathe new life into the doctrine of the Trinity by linking it with a "social programme." It is willing to risk the accusation of tritheism by pushing the social analogy of the Trinity as far as possible in order to present the communitarian life of egalitarian love between Father, Son, and Holy Spirit as the model for human society even within history: "The community of Father, Son and Holy Spirit becomes the prototype of the human community dreamed of by those who wish to improve society and build it in such a way as to make it into the image and likeness of the Trinity."[50]

Boff explores the political consequences of God-concepts and finds that "Absolutism," "Totalitarianism," and "Patriarchalism" are all supported by monarchial, monotheistic concepts of God. In other words, a proper social-critical analysis and hermeneutic of suspicion should lead to the conclusion that even Christians have constructed God-concepts to justify their preferred social orderings. The idea of divine monarchy (even "monarchy of the Father" within a weakly developed model of the Trinity) justifies hierarchical notions of human society in which emperors, kings, and dictators rule over all and men dominate women and children in families. Even in the church, Boff argues, dominance and oppression are intrinsically linked with certain ideas of God such that the Trinity itself is distorted to look like monarchial monotheism. Similarly, certain distorted ideas of the Trinity — generally based on speculation rather than revelation — serve to justify hierarchal models of society and church.

The Brazilian liberation theologian argues in *Trinity and Society* that what is needed is not only a radical reorientation of society "from below," so

50. Leonardo Boff, *Trinity and Society*, trans. Paul Burns (Maryknoll, N.Y.: Orbis, 1988), p. 7.

to speak, but also a theological vision of God that supports that egalitarian vision of human society as a community of equal brothers and sisters built on relationships of communion and participation rather than domination and oppression. The Christian socialist ideal of society, according to Boff, "is a pointer on the road to the mystery of the Trinity, while the mystery of the Trinity as we know it from revelation, is a pointer toward social life and its archetype."[51] Without naming the proper trinitarian archetype of the right ordering of society "the social analogy," that is exactly what Boff endorses and seeks to develop. He criticizes all theologians — including Barth and Rahner — who tend in any way to diminish the full distinct personal existences of the Father, Son, and Holy Spirit. Such quasi-modalistic reductions of the persons of the Trinity to mere modes of being or subsistences leads back to non-trinitarian monarchian monotheism, which in turn justifies social (including ecclesiastical) hierarchies. Drawing on the trinitarian reflections of German charismatic theologian Heribert Mühlen, Boff affirms the idea that persons always exist in relationships of "I-Thou-We" and never as isolated individuals with even multi-dimensional consciousnesses. Just as human persons exist in and for relationships, so God as personal exists in and for relationships. If God were not multi-personal, God would be impersonal or else the world would be necessary to God. And if there is hierarchy within the multi-personal being of the trinitarian community of God, then there is more than one god and that would be polytheism. The only alternative to these heresies, then, is to view God as the perfect community of co-equal persons.

How, then, are the three distinct persons of Father, Son, and Holy Spirit "one God" (one being, one *ousia*)? In order to explain this — something he must do to avoid tritheism — Boff turns to the ancient concept of "perichoresis" (Latin: *circumincessio*). The Eastern fathers of the church developed it to explain the *interpenetration* of the three persons of the Trinity. According to Boff, "each [person] is itself, not the other, but so open to the other and in the other that they form one entity, i.e., they are God."[52] Boff regards this *perichoretic* unity as *unity of love* and as *perfect personal communion* rather than as *unity of substance* or *unity of origin (Father)*. He believes that this kind of union within God provides the needed model for human societies even if no two or three human persons can ever

---

51. Boff, *Trinity and Society,* p. 119.
52. Boff, *Trinity and Society,* p. 32.

THE HISTORICAL DEVELOPMENT OF THE DOCTRINE

completely achieve such union. The triune being of God, then, is for Boff a fellowship of three distinct persons that can be at least weakly reflected in human societies: "Such an exchange of love obtains between the three Persons: life flows so completely between them, the communion between them is so infinite, with each bestowing on the others all that can be bestowed, that they form a union. The three possess one will, one understanding, one love."[53] This model of God, according to Boff, gives impetus to the revolutionary movement to make society and church (and family?) generators of greater participation, communion, and symmetry between human persons at all levels of human relationships.

Boff concludes that "society offends the Trinity" when it organizes itself on the basis of inequality and honors the Trinity when it organizes itself on the basis of sharing and communion between all persons and seeks to bring about justice and equality for all. Specifically, "The *church* is more the sacrament of trinitarian communion the more it reduces inequalities between Christians and between various ministries in it, and the more it understands and practices unity as co-existence in diversity."[54] The Brazilian theologian more than suggests that ultimately all the inequality between the Triune God and creation itself will be changed so that when God's purpose for salvation history is accomplished humanity and all creation will be "inserted into the very communion of Father, Son and Holy Spirit." The universe will be the "body of the Trinity." All inequalities that require power-over (dominance) will be changed into perfect communion. The utopian reality that characterizes the immanent Trinity will then also characterize the relationship between God and the world. In the meantime, Christians are called to do everything possible to approximate that utopia by abolishing dystopias marked by oppression of every kind.

If Leonardo Boff's main concern was to correct hierarchical notions of the Trinity in order to help deconstruct hierarchical organizations of society (including family and church), Catherine Mowry LaCugna's main concern in *God for Us: The Trinity and Christian Life* was to turn trinitarian reflection away from speculation on the immanent Trinity and God-in-himself toward reflection on the Trinity as the "mystery of salvation." That is, for her the *economic Trinity* should be the focus of Christian attention because it relates the triune being of God with salvation and

---

53. Boff, *Trinity and Society*, p. 84.
54. Boff, *Trinity and Society*, pp. 236-37.

Christian living. In fact, the Notre Dame professor went so far as to reject all abstract, speculative peering into the inner workings of the Trinity in heavenly eternity as the "defeat of the doctrine of the Trinity." Such speculation, she averred, is a debilitating habit of Christian thinking about God that must be overcome if trinitarian thought is to be related to real life, and if it is not related to real life it will become otiose. The immanent Trinity has too often been thought of as the "real Trinity" in contrast to God's economic trinitarian interactions with people in history. Contrary to this tendency, LaCugna wrote that

> If God is truly *self*-communicating, then we do know the essence (personal existence) of God: we know God as God truly is, in the mediation of God's self-revelation in Christ and the Spirit. The immanent Trinity is not transhistorical, transempirical, or transeconomic. Nor is the immanent Trinity a "more real" God — more real because the mode of discourse used to describe it is ontological. Rather, to speak about God in immanent trinitarian terms is nothing more than to speak about God's life with us in the economy of Christ and the Spirit.[55]

Of course, this is hardly how "immanent Trinity" has usually been described, but it is one possible interpretation of "Rahner's Rule," which links the immanent Trinity with the economic Trinity as closely and inextricably as possible. LaCugna's project was to carry "Rahner's Rule" to its *right* logical conclusion based on the insight that the inextricable link between them must not leave God needing the world to be triune while at the same time not disconnecting God-in-himself (immanent Trinity) from salvation history and experience.

Part One of *God for Us* presents a critical review of what LaCugna boldly calls "The Emergence and Defeat of the Doctrine of the Trinity." She surveys the development of trinitarian doctrine from the early church through the Constantinian and Augustinian eras through the Eastern and Western scholasticism of Gregory Palamas and Thomas Aquinas. The "story" that she tells is of the gradual decline of the concreteness of trinitarian reflection and its demise into abstraction and speculation. The ma-

---

55. Catherine Mowry LaCugna, *God for Us: The Trinity and Christian Life* (New York: HarperSanFrancisco, 1991), p. 229.

jor feature of that devolution is the dislocation between the economic Trinity, which reflects on God-for-us in the history of Father, Son, and Holy Spirit revealing and acting on behalf of humanity within salvation history, and the immanent Trinity, which refers to God's being-in-himself as the union-in-fellowship between Father, Son, and Holy Spirit. Very early in the history of theology reflection began to focus more and more on the immanent Trinity as church fathers became obsessed with Greek ideas of divine perfection and impassibility. Reluctance to allow any change or even suffering in God's being led to a separation between God's *being* and God's *revelation* outside himself. God *ad intra* (within himself) was described as triune but immutable and impassible, such that what happened *ad extra* (outside himself) could have no real effect on God in himself. Reflection on God-in-himself and the unchanging essential relationships between the triune persons became "theology proper" *(theologia),* and reflection on God-in-relation to the world and the missions and processions of the Son and Holy Spirit in incarnation, revelation, and redemption became "economy" *(economia)* and somehow less important in the task of constructing a Christian doctrine of God than theology proper. LaCugna makes a remarkable suggestion about a radically wrong twist in the narrative of the history of theology when she writes that "If Christian theology [in the works of Athanasius and the Cappadocian fathers] had let go the insistence on God's impassibility and affirmed that God suffers in Christ, it could have kept together, against Arianism, the essential unity and identity between the being of God and the being of Christ."[56] The effect of this separation between God's being-in-himself and God's being-in-Christ's suffering was an irrelevance of the doctrine of the immanent Trinity (which was treated as the "real Trinity") for Christian living in prayer, worship, and discipleship — an irrelevance that eventually led to neglect of the doctrine of the Trinity in Christian thought.

LaCugna's desire was to discover a way to establish and maintain an essential correlation between "economy" (the triune God *ad extra* in creation, incarnation, and redemption) and "theology proper" *(theologia)* that neither denies God's ontological freedom nor implies that the intradivine realm of persons lies completely on the other side of some ontological divide between God and the world. Part Two of *God for Us* is entitled "Re-Conceiving the Doctrine of the Trinity in Light of the Mystery of

---

56. LaCugna, *God for Us,* p. 43.

Salvation." The project of this second half of the book is to explore the following questions crucial to reconnecting the Trinity with real life:

> Can we affirm that God *as God* is altogether present in the economy of salvation history, and at the same time that God also exceeds and outstrips the human capacity to receive or explain this self-communication? Finally, is there a way to say that the specific modalities of God's self-communication in Christ and the Spirit are ineffable because they show us the true nature of God, without appealing to "intradivine" relations or "intradivine" self-communication?[57]

LaCugna is convinced that the answer to both questions is "Yes" and that the key to such an answer is to reconceive the immanent Trinity *as* the economic Trinity without dissolving God in the world. But this can only be accomplished by abolishing the traditional notions of God's immutability and impassibility which caused the problem revealed in Part One of *God for Us*. For LaCugna even the concept of immanent Trinity must be changed so that it does not refer to some "interior and eternal life of God apart from the world" but refers instead to "God revealed in Christ and the Spirit." "An immanent trinitarian theology, in other words, cannot be an analysis of what is 'inside' God, but a way of thinking and speaking about the structure or pattern of God's self-expression in salvation history."[58] In the final analysis, then, for LaCugna, *God is who and what he is among us in Christ and the Spirit*. There is no immanent Trinity in the traditional sense. What remains of the immanent Trinity? Doxology. That is, we are to praise God — who is radically free and relates historically with the world graciously and not by necessity — while refusing to speculate about how it is the case that God is both historical and free. LaCugna dares to ask and refuses to answer *the crucial question for classical trinitarian theism:* "Would God be triune apart from the economy of salvation history?" She writes: "As soon as we leave the economy behind, the doctrine of the Trinity has no bearing on life or faith. This is the import of [the] point that the question of whether God would be trinitarian apart from salvation history is purely speculative and cannot be answered on the basis of revelation."[59]

---

57. LaCugna, *God for Us*, p. 217.
58. LaCugna, *God for Us*, p. 225.
59. LaCugna, *God for Us*, p. 227.

Thus, the immanent triune being of Father, Son, and Holy Spirit *is* their relationships with each other and with humans in the process of salvation history that begins with creation and has no ending. The distinction between "immanent Trinity" and "economic Trinity" is for LaCugna, then, *not ontological* but *doxological*. That is, it does not refer to two distinct "beings of God" but only to a necessary worshipful acknowledgment of God's holy freedom over against necessity or compulsion in his self-expression as Father, Son, and Holy Spirit in the world.

Critics have wondered whether LaCugna has done justice to the freedom of God which is necessary for the graciousness of God's redemptive presence in Christ and through the Holy Spirit in the church and the world. Is it necessary wholly to abolish all ontological distinction between immanent Trinity and economic Trinity in order to preserve the relevance of the Trinity for Christian life? Or might some bare acknowledgment be necessary that Father, Son, and Holy Spirit have a life of their own in eternity not exhausted by their economic self-expression and redemptive activities in salvation history? Does LaCugna inadvertently exchange one value for another one when both must be preserved? That is, does her insistence on *relevance of the Trinity for Christian life* (prayer, spirituality, worship) lead her to undermine the *total gratuity of grace* by making God a prisoner (as it were) of history? Might it not serve both values if one said that "once there is a world" (based entirely on God's gracious decision to create something outside himself) there is no ontological "distance" between immanent and economic Trinities? The immanent Trinity, then, would refer only to God's "previous" existence "before and apart from the world," and the "immanent-economic Trinity" would refer to God's self-expression toward the world and in the world. One could exchange "pre-historical" and "historical" for the qualifiers "immanent" and "economic" and have the same effect.

Although Eastern Orthodox theologian John D. Zizioulas's treatise *Being As Communion: Studies in Personhood and the Church* was not at first greeted as a constructive contribution to the doctrine of the Trinity when it was published in 1985, it began to influence Christian reflection on the Trinity in the early 1990s and therefore represents in some ways the culmination of trinitarian thought in the second millennium and twentieth century. Little was known of Zizioulas before the publication and reception of this important investigation of the relationships between being, Trinity, personhood, the church, and the future. At the time of the book's publication the author was professor of systematic theology at the University of Glasgow in Scotland and had previously lectured at the Gregorian University in Rome and at King's College in London. According to his publisher, Zizioulas has been a major Orthodox contributor to modern ecumenical discussions.

In *Being As Communion* Zizioulas presents a tightly packed and highly nuanced argument in favor of the Eastern patristic consensus about the doctrine of the Trinity as the only viable alternative to pantheism and nihilism. This he does by exploring the nature of personhood in both God and humanity. A non-trinitarian creator God would need a world as his counterpart because personhood is a mystery of relationship. There is no non-relational person. The modern dilemma of personhood is that by emphasizing self-existence in freedom as the true essence of personhood the question of suicide as the ultimate expression of freedom and therefore of self-actualization cannot be avoided or answered. According to Zizioulas, the Eastern non-catechetical church fathers (i.e., bishops such as Irenaeus and Athanasius) understood the nature of personhood and its relationship to "substance" more profoundly than any ancient or modern thinkers. In contrast to the Greek philosophers and even the Alexandrian catechetical Christian theologians (Clement of Alexandria and Origen) the trinitarian fathers of the East elevated the category of "person" to highest ontological status while at the same time envisioning it as real only in relationship. God as triune, they argued, is fully personal, and the divine substance *(ousia)* is the personhood of God. To be God is to be personal and to be personal is to exist in and for communion.

Zizioulas's favorite phrase for ultimate reality is "ecclesial being" or "ecclesial identity," and he asserts that "ecclesial being is bound to the very being of God," that God's being is an "event of communion."[60] The author protests the tendency of Western Christianity to elevate divine and human substances above personhood. This tendency, he argues, has led to Western individualism and the modern dilemma of nihilistic selfhood. Against that Western tendency he asserts that even for God, person precedes being or that being *is* person and that person *is* communion. The Eastern fathers' great contribution to the history of thought lies precisely in their insight that even "The substance of God, 'God', has no ontological content, no

60. John D. Zizioulas, *Being As Communion: Studies in Personhood and the Church* (Crestwood, N.Y.: St. Vladimir's Press, 1984), p. 15.

true being, apart from communion."[61] According to Zizioulas, this by no means implies a strict equality of the trinitarian persons, however. Even though the communion that God *is* is triune as Father, Son, and Holy Spirit, there is a common source of that communion — the Father, who is the mystery of pure person per se. "Thus, God as person — as the hypostasis of the Father — makes the one divine substance to be that which it is: the one God."[62] The Son and Holy Spirit are eternally bound with the Father as their common source and together with the Father form a perfect divine community of which the church — at its best — is an icon (image). There is no God prior to or apart from or above Father as person, and there is no Father-person apart from eternal communion between Father and Son and Holy Spirit. To be God is to be perfect communion between persons and to be human is to exist in communion that reflects that perfect divine communion.

Zizioulas does not intend to present some novel or innovative reconstruction of the doctrine of the Trinity. Rather, in *Being As Communion* he is calling Christian theological and ontological reflection back to a source almost forgotten, especially in the West: the Greek patristic tradition of the formative fourth century — the century in which Athanasius and the Cappadocian fathers achieved a momentous breakthrough not only in the realm of Christian doctrine but also in the sphere of philosophy. The highest being, they claimed, is not isolated self-sufficiency of pure substance, nor is it all-oneness of monistic pantheism. It is rather personhood: "ecclesial being," which exists in and for others. Thus, love rather than self-sufficiency or self-assertion is the true mode of being. To be is to love others. This is only true, Zizioulas reminds his readers, if there is a God who embodies this in himself and in whose image and likeness we humans are made.

One does have to wonder whether the "monarchy of the Father" that remains in Zizioulas's trinitarian program of reform-by-return-to-tradition is consistent with his basic communitarian impulses. Could not one rather interpret the monarchy of the Father to justify "benevolent despotism"? Certainly Zizioulas is not arguing for a complete egalitarianism anyway. However, many Western communitarian thinkers who have strong sympathies with the Eastern tradition of placing person over sub-

---

61. Zizioulas, *Being As Communion*, p. 17.
62. Zizioulas, *Being As Communion*, p. 41.

stance (e.g., Moltmann) will wonder whether the Eastern Orthodox theologian has really carried out his program consistently. Nevertheless, Zizioulas's emphasis on pure personhood as being prior to substance in the ontological scheme and on pure personhood as communion is a welcome correction to so much modern, Western individualism, and it appears as a welcome Eastern Orthodox contribution to the twentieth-century renaissance of the doctrine of the Trinity.

Discussion and explication of the Trinity may never truly cease, yet we have come now to the end of our story. Indeed, we find that it has come full circle, back to its classical origins. The doctrine, however difficult of exposition, will continue to fascinate theologians. For in it, in the very mystery of the Trinity, the discussion may well come to embrace the fullness of God's existence, and of our own.

ANNOTATED BIBLIOGRAPHY

3. Bibliography of English Language
Works on the Trinity

This annotated bibliography of books is selective according to three main criteria. First, in order to be included here a work must be significant in terms of its contribution to the development of the doctrine of the Trinity. Minor and most secondary works (e.g., surveys) are excluded. Second, in order to be included here a work must be relatively readily available either by purchase order or through libraries (including interlibrary loan). Third, in order to be included here works must be in English translation. There are, of course, many chapters on the doctrine of the Trinity in theological volumes that fit these three criteria, but most volumes of systematic theology that include only a chapter or section on the Trinity are excluded here. Some patristic volumes are included that only contain portions on the Trinity because of their seminal importance in the early development of the doctrine.

1. Patristic Resources

Abbreviations

ACW   Ancient Christian Writers: The Works of the Fathers in Translation. Mahwah, N.J.: Paulist, 1946-.

ANF   A. Roberts and J. Donaldson, eds. Ante-Nicene Fathers. 10 vols. Buffalo, N.Y.: Christian Literature, 1885-1896. Reprint, Grand Rapids: Eerdmans, 1951-1956. Reprint, Peabody, Mass.: Hendrickson, 1994.

FC   R. J. Deferrari, ed. Fathers of the Church: A New Translation. Washington, D.C.: Catholic University of America Press, 1947-.

LCC   J. Baillie et al., eds. The Library of Christian Classics. 26 vols. Philadelphia: Westminster, 1953-1966.

NPNF   P. Schaff et al., eds. A Select Library of the Nicene and Post-Nicene Fathers of the Christian Church, series 1 and 2 (14 vols. each). Buffalo, N.Y.: Christian Literature, 1887-1894. Reprint, Edinburgh, T. & T. Clark; Grand Rapids: Eerdmans, 1952-1956. Reprint, Peabody, Mass.: Hendrickson, 1994.

Early Ante-Nicene Contributions

In this section we direct our attention to Christian writers working in the late first and early second century, often referred to as the Apostolic Fathers (ca. 70-135 CE). Significant communal documents produced in the Ante-Nicene period are also listed. For a revised and edited translation of relevant Ante-Nicene material, consult *The Apostolic Fathers,* second edition, translated by J. B. Lightfoot and J. R. Harmer, edited and revised by Michael W. Holmes (Grand Rapids: Baker Book House, 1989).

Clement. *1 Clement.* Translated by J. B. Lightfoot and J. R. Harmer. Edited and revised by Michael W. Holmes. Included in *The Apostolic Fathers,* pp. 28-64. Quite possibly the earliest extant Christian document outside the canon of the New Testament. We encounter no developed trinitarian reflection in this early episcopal letter, but do find repeated references to the Father, Son, and Holy Spirit. At this early stage in the tradition 1 Clement contains statements with startling trinitarian implications. Firmer trinitarian affirmations will come later.

2 Clement. Translated by J. B. Lightfoot and J. R. Harmer. Edited and revised by Michael W. Holmes. Included in *The Apostolic Fathers,* pp. 68-78. Michael Holmes writes that *2 Clement* is "the oldest complete Christian sermon that has survived." Its authorship, date, and occasion are largely a mystery. The first line of the sermon immediately catches the eye and ear: "Brothers, we ought to think of Jesus Christ, as we do of God, as 'judge of the living and the dead.'"

Constitutions of the Holy Apostles. Edited by James Donaldson. ANF 7 (Peabody, Mass.: Hendrickson, 1994). Section 4, chapter 41, contains a very interesting statement of the creed recited by catechumens at the time of their baptism. Its trinitarian structure is striking. Chapter 43, describing the blessing pronounced over the waters of baptism, is also highly trinitarian in its language and structure. The prayers contained in book 8, chapters 5-11, 13-15, 17-20, 35-41, should also be consulted. Cf. also the *Early Liturgies* contained in ANF 7, pp. 537-68.

Hermas. *The Shepherd of Hermas.* Translated by J. B. Lightfoot and J. R. Harmer. Edited and revised by Michael W. Holmes. Included in *The Apostolic Fathers*, pp. 194-290. An early Christian document that illustrates the difficulty Christian writers faced in making sense out of the biblical data concerning the Father, Son, and Holy Spirit. Helpful for readers interested in the common mistakes early Christian thinkers sometimes made in their attempts to form adequate theological models for the complex first-century witness to the gospel.

Ignatius. *Letter to the Ephesians.* Translated by J. B. Lightfoot and J. R. Harmer. Edited and revised by Michael W. Holmes. Included in *The Apostolic Fathers*, pp. 86-93. Ignatius, bishop of Antioch, authored seven letters to various churches (i.e., Smyrna, Philadelphia, Ephesus) as he was led under Roman guard to execution in Rome. The letter to the church in Ephesus should particularly be consulted.

Lactantius. *Divine Institutes.* Translated by William Fletcher. ANF 7 (Peabody, Mass.: Hendrickson, 1994). Readers should peruse book 4. Lactantius addresses numerous christological questions here, and in chapter 23 explores the relationship between Father and Son, using the common patristic illustrations of fountain and stream, sun and sunlight. Cf. also Lantantius, *The Epitome of the Divine Institutes*, ANF 7, chapters 43-47, 49-51.

The Apocrypha: The Book of John Concerning the Falling Asleep of Mary. Translated by Alexander Walker. ANF 8 (Peabody, Mass.: Hendrickson, 1994). One of many apocryphal books commenting on silent aspects of the New Testament, i.e., events ignored by New Testament writers such as the death of Mary. While this short work contains no explicit trinitarian reflection, it is noteworthy as an interesting example of how early Christians spoke of the Father, Christ, and the Holy Spirit. John and Mary, for example, repeatedly refer to Jesus as "Christ our God," "God the Lord," and "God her Savior."

The Didache. Translated by J. B. Lightfoot and J. R. Harmer. Edited and revised by Michael W. Holmes. Included in *The Apostolic Fathers*, pp. 149-

58. A helpful example of early Christian catechesis; that is, a theological and devotional handbook of sorts for instructing early Christian converts in the faith. Although sparse in its trinitarian witness, the implications of *The Didache's* language surely help to nudge the church in a trinitarian direction.

The Epistle of Barnabas. Translated by J. B. Lightfoot and J. R. Harmer. Edited and revised by Michael W. Holmes. Included in *The Apostolic Fathers,* pp. 162-88. An early Christian writer sifts through the pages of the Hebrew scriptures, searching for texts illustrating the fulfillment of God's purposes in Christ. Some interesting christological insights. Less said on the Holy Spirit.

The Martyrdom of Polycarp. Translated by J. B. Lightfoot and J. R. Harmer. Edited and revised by Michael W. Holmes. Included in *The Apostolic Fathers,* pp. 135-44. An extremely moving account of the martyrdom of the faithful bishop Polycarp. Again, as in other Ante-Nicene texts, readers should focus on the implications of the language used to narrate Polycarp's story. The writer of the narrative is clearly not producing a trinitarian treatise, yet employs language that will catch the attention of alert readers mining for trinitarian nuggets.

Theognostus of Alexandria. *From His Seven Books of Hypotyposes or Outlines.* Translated by S. D. F. Salmond. ANF 6 (Peabody, Mass.: Hendrickson, 1994). Three extremely short fragments from a larger work. All three fragments deal with trinitarian questions such as the "substance" of the Son in relationship to the "substance" of the Father. The common illustration of the sun and its rays also appears.

Athenagoras. *A Plea for the Christians.* Translated by B. P. Pratten. ANF 2 (Peabody, Mass.: Hendrickson, 1994). A helpful example of early Ante-Nicene reflection on the Trinity. Athenagoras argues that it is not at all irrational to assert that the one God might have a Son. Athenagoras could be clearer on the generation of the Son. Is the Son eternally distinct from the Father, or does he become so at creation when God utters his Word? The distinct personality of the Spirit is cloudy in Athenagoras, as his description of the Spirit as an "effluence" hints. For a relatively recent translation of *A Plea for the Christians,* cf. Athenagoras, *Embassy for the Christians,* translated by Joseph Hugh Crehan, S.J. (New York: Paulist Press, 1955).

Justin Martyr. *Dialogue with Trypho.* Edited by Alexander Roberts and James Donaldson. ANF 1 (Peabody, Mass.: Hendrickson, 1994). Justin responds to Jewish objections to the possibility that Jesus of Nazareth could be the promised Messiah and also divine in nature. Chapters 55-66, 83-85, deal directly with the question of Christ's divinity, its implications for his relationship with the Father, and its relationship to Christ's life as a genuine human being. Cf. also *Selections from Justin Martyr's Dialogue with Trypho, a Jew,* translated by R. P. C. Hanson, World Christian Books 49, third series (London: Lutterworth, 1963).

—————. *First Apology* and *Second Apology.* Edited by Alexander Roberts and James Donaldson. ANF 1 (Peabody, Mass.: Hendrickson, 1994). The *First Apology* contains similar arguments to those contained in the *Dialogue with Trypho.* Justin is foggy on the eternal nature of the Son and at times conflates the Spirit with the *Logos.* For example, in the *First Apology* he writes that "it is wrong . . . to understand the Spirit and the power of God as anything else than the Word, who is also the first-born of God" (*First Apology* 33.6).

Tatian. *Address to the Greeks.* Translated by J. E. Ryland. ANF 2 (Peabody, Mass.: Hendrickson, 1994). Tatian strongly belittles Greek culture, religion, and philosophy. In the first section (chapters 4.3–7.6) we receive a taste of Tatian's cosmology and understanding of God. He compares the relationship between God and the *Logos* to that of a torch and the light it produces. Tatian, like Justin, seems confused regarding the generation of the Son; he speaks of the *Logos* as begotten of God, but does not appear to understand the generation of the Son as an eternal generation (cf. ch. 5).

Theophilus of Antioch. *Theophilus to Autolycus.* ANF 2 (Peabody, Mass.: Hendrickson, 1994). Theophilus, a second-century bishop of Antioch, is quite similar to other Ante-Nicene apologists in his trinitarian ideas. He is, however, the first Christian theologian to make the distinction between the *Logos endiathetos* (the immanent Word) and the *Logos prophorikos* (the Word "emitted"). Theophilus' comments on the Spirit are relatively sparse and occasionally he blurs the distinction between the Word and the Spirit (cf. book 2, ch. 10). Theophilus' reference to the Trinity *(triados)* in his correspondence with Autolycus is perhaps the earliest patristic use of the term.

Early Alexandrian Contributions

Clement of Alexandria. *The Instructor (Paidagogos)*. ANF 2 (Peabody, Mass.: Hendrickson, 1994). Clement's "Prayer to the Paedagogus" is a fine example of an early Christian petition and doxology to the Father, Son, and Holy Spirit.

―――. *Stromata*. ANF 2 (Peabody, Mass.: Hendrickson, 1994). Clement speaks of the Trinity as reflected in Plato's *Timaeus*. In book 7, chapter 2, Clement reflects on the relationship between the Father and Son, writing that the "Son of God is never displaced; not being divided, not severed, not passing from place to place; being always everywhere, and being contained nowhere, complete mind, the complete paternal mind . . . the paternal word, exhibiting the holy administration for Him who put [all] in subjection to Him" (ANF 2, book 7, p. 524). For a recent translation of the first three books of the *Stromata*, cf. Clement of Alexandria, *Stromateis*, translated by John Ferguson, FC 85 (Washington, D.C.: Catholic University of America Press, 1991).

―――. "Who Is the Rich Man That Shall Be Saved?" Translated by William Wilson. ANF 2 (Peabody, Mass.: Hendrickson, 1994). A sermon that contains Clement's comment on the protection offered by "the power of God the Father, and the blood of God the Son, and the dew of the Holy Spirit" (ANF 2, para. 34, p. 601).

Dionysius of Alexandria. Translated by S. D. F. Salmond. *Epistle to Dionysius Bishop of Rome*. ANF 6 (Peabody, Mass.: Hendrickson, 1994). While only fragments of Dionysius' work are available in English, readers would do well to study the extracts from Dionysius' letter to Dionysius of Rome in which he clarifies earlier comments he had made in response to Sabellian tendencies in the Pentapolis. Apparently Dionysius of Alexandria had so stressed the distinctiveness of the divine persons that he was misunderstood to be heading in the direction of tritheism. In the fragments of his explanatory letter to Dionysius of Rome he explains more thoroughly his position. While maintaining the distinctiveness of the persons Dionysius insists that they are inseparable and consubstantial. Extracts from the first and second books of this epistle provide excellent illustrations of Ante-Nicene trinitarian thinking and language.

Dionysius of Rome. *Against the Sabellians*. Translated by William Fletcher. ANF 7 (Peabody, Mass.: Hendrickson, 1994). An Ante-Nicene work written against "the opinion of Sabellius," who erred in arguing "that the Son Himself is the Father, and *vice versa*" (ANF 7, p. 365). This is a work known by Athanasius. He includes its ideas in his own response to Arian and Sabellian positions.

Origen. *On First Principles (De Principiis).* Translated by Frederick Crombie. ANF 4 (Peabody, Mass.: Hendrickson, 1994). A work that contains important and interesting examples of a great exegete and theologian's attempt to understand the biblical testimony to the Father, Son, and Spirit. Origen is not always correct in his musings and constructions, but his contributions to trinitarian reflection cannot be ignored. Note particularly Origen's preface, section 4; book 1, chapter 1, "on God," chapter 2, "on Christ," and chapter 3, "on the Holy Spirit." Book 2 should also be consulted, especially chapter 4 (on the identity of the God of the Old Testament and the Father of Jesus Christ), chapter 6 (on the incarnation of Christ), and chapter 7 (on the Holy Spirit). Book 4 contains a nice summary "regarding the Father, the Son, and the Holy Spirit" (ANF 4, book 4, pp. 376-82). Cf. also Origen, *On First Principles,* translated by G. W. Butterworth (London: SPCK, 1936; reprint, Gloucester, Mass.: Peter Smith, 1973).

————. *Against Celsus.* Translated by Frederick Crombie. ANF 4 (Peabody, Mass.: Hendrickson, 1994). Readers will probably find book 8, chapters 12-15, to be of most interest. Here Origen replies to Celsus' assertion that Christians worship not only God but "servants" of God. Origen's response falls short of the mark of complete consistency and orthodoxy. He asserts that the Son is "inferior" to the Father, while simultaneously arguing that the Father and Son, "two persons," are both worshiped by the Christian community. Cf. also Origen, *Contra Celsum,* translated by Henry Chadwick (Cambridge: Cambridge University Press, 1953).

————. *Commentary on John.* Translated by Allan Menzies. ANF 9 (Peabody, Mass.: Hendrickson, 1994). Origen's exegesis of the first chapter of John's gospel is particularly important (ANF 9, pp. 305-39). Origen's exegesis is not always convincing, but his struggle to make sense out of the relationship between the Word, the Spirit, and the Father remain must reading for those who would understand later trinitarian developments.

Early Western Contributions

Cyprian. *On the Unity of the Church.* Translated by Ernest Wallis. ANF 5 (Peabody, Mass.: Hendrickson, 1994). Cyprian writes that the schism initiated by Novatian over the forgiveness and re-admission of those who have lapsed during persecution violates the principle of a more fundamental unity, that between the Father, Son, and Holy Spirit.

———. *Three Books of Testimonies Against the Jews.* Translated by Ernest Wallis. ANF 5 (Peabody, Mass.: Hendrickson, 1994). An example of an early church father employing Scripture to respond to specific issues pertaining to Christians and Jews. Jewish opponents of the Christian faith were concerned for the unity of God and could not understand how the affirmation of Christ's deity preserved this unity. Hence, Cyprian addresses a number of christological questions inextricably linked to trinitarian concepts, including the crucial question of Christ's deity.

Irenaeus. *Against Heresies.* ANF 1 (Peabody, Mass.: Hendrickson, 1994). Irenaeus' thought remains the most significant Christian response to gnostic ideas in the late second century CE. In light of the many modern gnosticisms, some of which have appeared in Christian garb, a close inspection of Irenaeus' thinking and its trinitarian implications is well worth the effort. Irenaeus' comments on theological methodology alone make this work invaluable. In response to the gnostics' inflated claims to knowledge of divine mysteries, Irenaeus reminds his readers that a human being "is infinitely inferior to God . . . he cannot have experience or form a conception of all things like God. . . . Preserve therefore the proper order of your knowledge, and do not, as being ignorant of things really good, seek to rise above God himself" (ANF 1, book 2.25.3-4). Paulist Press is producing a modern translation of *Against Heresies.* The first volume was published in 1992. Cf. St. Irenaeus of Lyons, *Against the Heresies,* translated by Dominic J. Unger, O.F.M. CAP, vol. 1 (New York: Paulist Press, 1992).

———. *Fragments from the Lost Writings of Irenaeus.* ANF 1 (Peabody, Mass.: Hendrickson, 1994). The three fragments remaining from this work are largely christological in nature and represent well Irenaeus' consistent argument that the Father and Son are one God, not two, and surely not part of a chain of aeons or angels as gnostic teachers believed and taught.

126

————. *Proof of the Apostolic Preaching.* Translated by Joseph P. Smith, S.J. (New York: Newman Press, n.d.). A much shorter and succinct presentation of Irenaeus' thinking, including key trinitarian comments and reflections. Note especially section 5, "The Trinity and Creatures," section 7, "The Trinity and Our Rebirth," and section 99, "Error Against the Persons of the Trinity." Also available in a very helpful translation by John Behr from St. Vladimir's Press. Cf. St. Irenaeus of Lyons, *On the Apostolic Preaching,* translated by John Behr (Crestwood, N.Y.: St. Vladimir's Press, 1997).

Hippolytus. *Against the Heresy of One Noetus.* ANF 5 (Peabody, Mass.: Hendrickson, 1994). Hippolytus responds to Noetus, a native of Smyrna who argued that Christ was actually the Father incarnate. Hippolytus is somewhat similar to Theophilus of Antioch in the distinction he makes between the immanent Word *(logos endiathetos)* and the Word manifested when the Father creates the universe *(logos prophorikos)*. He is clear in his understanding of the personal distinction between the Father and Son, but less so regarding the personal distinctiveness of the Holy Spirit.

————. *Against Beron and Helix.* ANF 5 (Peabody, Mass.: Hendrickson, 1994). A short treatise, largely focusing on the relationship between the divine and human nature of Christ, but with trinitarian implications.

Novatian. *A Treatise of Novatian Concerning the Trinity.* Translated by Robert Ernest Wallis. ANF 5 (Peabody, Mass.: Hendrickson, 1994). Cf. also Novatian, *The Trinity,* translated by Russell J. DeSimone, FC 67 (Washington, D.C.: Catholic University of America Press, 1974). A significant example of Ante-Nicene trinitarian reflection. Novatian ponders Christ's divinity, the relationship between the Father and Son and the nature of their distinction, and the nature and work of the Holy Spirit. Students interested in the Sabellian controversy will find this treatise especially helpful. Novatian attacks both Sabellius' modalism — the idea that the Father, Son, and Spirit are actually God assuming three roles or wearing three masks — and bi-theism, the concept that Christians worship two gods, the Father and Son. Novatian struggles to make sense of the generation of the Son and seems to assert that the Son is in some sense "born." Subordinationist tendencies occur in Novatian's thought, a trend not uncommon in Ante-Nicene writers.

Tertullian. *Against Praxeas.* Translated by Peter Holmes. ANF 3 (Peabody, Mass.: Hendrickson, 1994). A highly significant early trinitarian treatise judged by Johannes Quasten to be "the most important contribution to the doctrine of the Trinity in the Ante-Nicene period." Tertullian discusses unity and distinction within the Trinity, popular misconceptions of the doctrine, and the relation between the Father and Son. He also addresses the person of the Holy Spirit and the nature of the Spirit's subsistence. This is an interesting treatise, especially because of Tertullian's detailed discussion of biblical passages that underlie the church's growing apprehension of the trinitarian nature of God.

————. *Apology.* Translated by S. Thelwall. ANF 3 (Peabody, Mass.: Hendrickson, 1994). Chapter 21 of the *Apology* contains a helpful example of third-century CE language concerning the relationship of the Father and Son. Again the illustration of the sun and its rays appears. "Even when the ray is shot from the sun, it is still part of the parent mass; the sun will still be in the ray, because it is a ray of the sun — there is no division of substance, but merely an extension. Thus Christ is Spirit of Spirit, and God of God, as light of light is kindled" (*Apology*, p. 34).

————. *Against Marcion.* Translated by Peter Holmes. ANF 3 (Peabody, Mass.: Hendrickson, 1994). Contains a valuable discussion of God's unity (book 1, chapters 3-7, pp. 273-76).

————. *On the Flesh of Christ.* Translated by Peter Holmes. ANF 3 (Peabody, Mass.: Hendrickson, 1994). Consult chapter 18 for Tertullian's response to the question: "Did Jesus possess a genuine human body?"

Key Eastern Figures from the Age of Nicea and Beyond

Alexander of Alexandria. *Epistles on the Arian Heresy and the Deposition of Arius.* Translated by James B. H. Hawkins. ANF 6 (Peabody, Mass.: Hendrickson, 1994). Letters and documents illustrating the outbreak and response to the Arian controversy, a theological dispute destined to rage for most of the fourth century CE.

Arius. *Thalia.* Sections preserved in Athanasius, *Four Discourses Against the Arians.* Translated by J. H. Newman, NPNF Second Series 4 (Peabody, Mass.: Hendrickson, 1994). The teaching of Arius, the main theological antagonist of "orthodoxy" in the fourth century CE, is only available in quotations, almost all from his opponents. Although we cannot be absolutely sure of Arius' exact words, we can be confident that he had great difficulty in understanding how the Son could share divinity with the Father. Arius proposed that the Son was an exalted creature, elevated above all others, but still a creation of God. It is the thought of Arius and the necessity of responding to it that spawns the rich christological theology of the fourth century and, towards its conclusion, much needed exploration of the person and work of the Holy Spirit. For examples of direct quotations by Athanasius from Arius' *Thalia,* cf. Athanasius, *Four Discourses Against the Arians,* Discourse 1, chapter 2.

Athanasius. *Four Discourses Against the Arians.* Translated by J. H. Newman. NPNF Second Series 4 (Peabody, Mass.: Hendrickson, 1994). Athanasius' exegesis and theology are inseparably linked to his lifelong battle with Arianism. These four discourses, translated by Cardinal Newman, deal with close to every aspect of the Arian controversy, and also introduce us to the indomitable, often irascible bishop of Alexandria.

————. *On the Incarnation.* Intro. C. S. Lewis (Crestwood, N.Y.: St. Vladimir's Press, 1982). C. S. Lewis comments in his introduction to this great work that "this is a good translation of a very great book. St. Athanasius stood *contra mundum* for the Trinitarian doctrine 'whole and undefiled,' when it looked as if all the civilized world was slipping back from Christianity into the religion of Arius, into one of those 'sensible' synthetic religions which are so strongly recommended today . . . when I first opened his *De Incarnatione* I soon discovered by a very simple test that I was reading a masterpiece, for only a master could have written so deeply on such a subject with such classical simplicity." Enough said.

Basil the Great. *Letters.* Translated by Roy J. Deferrari (Cambridge, Mass.: Harvard University Press, 1986). Basil sprinkled sparkling trinitarian insights throughout his correspondence. Four volumes of Basil's letters have been translated by Roy J. Deferrari and published in the Loeb Classical Library. Catholic University of America Press has also published a collection of Basil's letters. Cf. Basil, *Letters,* translated by Sister Agnes Clare Way, FC 28 (Washington, D.C.: Catholic University of America Press, 1955).

————. *On the Holy Spirit.* Translated by David Anderson (Crestwood, N.Y.: St. Vladimir's Press, 1980). Cf. also Saint Basil the Great, *The Treatise de Spiritu Sancto,* translated by Blomfield Jackson, NPNF Second Series 8 (Peabody, Mass.: Hendrickson, 1994). A work filled with insight concerning the Spirit's relationship to the Father and Son. Basil develops his case for the Spirit's divinity by focusing on the implications of the work of the Spirit for the person of the Spirit. That is, if the activities of the Spirit are possessed in common with the Father and Son, must not the Spirit possess the same common nature?

Cyril of Alexandria. *On the Unity of Christ*. Translated by John Anthony McGuckin (Crestwood, N.Y.: St. Vladimir's Press, 1995). A work more christological than trinitarian in its focus, but still filled with significant trinitarian implications. Readers interested in primary data concerning the Nestorian controversy will find Cyril's treatise valuable. Letter 55 in St. Cyril of Alexandria, *Letters 51-110*, translated by John I. McEnerney, FC 77 (Washington, D.C.: Catholic University of America Press, 1987), also contains a succinct summary of Cyril's christology.

Cyril of Jerusalem. *Catechetical Lectures*. Translated by Edwin Hamilton Gifford. NPNF Second Series 7 (Peabody, Mass.: Hendrickson, 1994). Cf. also *The Works of Saint Cyril of Jerusalem*, translated by Leo P. McCauley, S.J., and Anthony A. Stephenson, FC 1 (Washington, D.C.: Catholic University of America Press, 1969); *The Works of Saint Cyril of Jerusalem*, translated by Leo P. McCauley, S.J., and Anthony A. Stephenson, FC 2 (Washington, D.C.: Catholic University of America Press, 1970). Cyril of Jerusalem represents well those fathers who had reservations concerning the use of the term *homoousion* to describe the shared essence of Father, Son, and Spirit, and yet strongly supported the biblical testimony concerning the deity of all three persons. When Cyril became convinced that the new language and model offered by Nicea was faithful to the testimony of the Scripture, he clearly indicated his support for these key creeds.

Saint Gregory of Nazianzus. *Select Orations*. Translated by Charles Gordon Browne and James Edward Swallow. NPNF Second Series 7 (Peabody, Mass.: Hendrickson, 1994). Gregory served for a short but extremely crucial period as bishop of Constantinople at the close of the heated era of the Arian controversy. During this time he preached a series of homilies attacking the rampant Arianism present in Constantinople. In these orations Gregory defends the deity of both the Son and the Holy Spirit, proposing the idea of progressive revelation as a helpful concept in understanding the development of the doctrine of the Trinity. Particular attention should be given to the fifth theological oration, in which Gregory focuses on the Holy Spirit. A number of key orations are included in *Christology of the Later Fathers*, edited by Edward Hardy, LCC

(Philadelphia: Westminster Press, 1954). Cf. also F. W. Norris, *Faith Gives Fullness to Reasoning: The Five Theological Orations of Gregory Nazianzen* (Leiden and New York: E. J. Brill, 1991).

Gregory of Nyssa. *On "Not Three Gods." To Ablabius.* Translated by H. A. Wilson. NPNF Second Series 5 (Peabody, Mass.: Hendrickson, 1994). Gregory is concerned to explain the nature of God's unity and why a nature shared between Father, Son, and Spirit must not lead to the conclusion that the Trinity is in reality three gods. Volume 5 of the NPNF contains a wide selection of Gregory's writings, including *On the Holy Trinity, and of the Godhead of the Holy Spirit; On the Holy Spirit: Against the Followers of Macedonius; Against Eunomius;* and *Answer to Eunomius' Second Book.*

John of Damascus. *Exposition of the Orthodox Faith.* Translated by S. D. F. Salmond. NPNF Second Series 9 (Peabody, Mass.: Hendrickson, 1994). A brief but comprehensive treatment of Greek trinitarian thought. Among other things, John's work illustrates well how the church's understanding of the Holy Spirit over the three centuries since Nicea (325 CE) and Constantinople (381 CE) has developed and matured.

Key Latin Contributions

Ambrose. *On the Christian Faith.* In *Some of the Principal Works of St. Ambrose.* Translated by H. De Romestin, NPNF Second Series 10 (Peabody, Mass.: Hendrickson, 1994). In defense of the Trinity against its various opponents, Ambrose deals with a number of key topics and issues including the nature of the unity between the Father and Son, the deity of the Son, Christ's eternity, the nature of the divine generation, the various names of the Son, and the purpose of the incarnation. Throughout the work Ambrose exegetes a number of biblical passages, especially centering on texts Arians employed in their argument that the Son was an exalted creature, but not God.

———. *On the Holy Spirit.* In *Some of the Principal Works of St. Ambrose,* op. cit. *On the Christian Faith* and *On the Holy Spirit* were sometimes grouped together as a single work, *On the Trinity (De Trinitate),* though it is highly probable that *On the Christian Faith* is the earlier of the two works. Both are indispensable for understanding Latin trinitarian theology. It is in *On the Holy Spirit* that Ambrose offers his famous four marks of the "glory of the Godhead": God's sinlessness, God's right and power to forgive sins, God as creator, and God as the proper object of all worship.

Augustine. *City of God.* Translated by Henry Bettenson (New York: Penguin Books, 1984). Cf. also Augustine, *City of God,* translated by Marcus Dods, NPNF First Series 2 (Peabody, Mass.: Hendrickson, 1994). The following sections should be particularly consulted: book 11, chapter 10 ("In the Trinity quality and substance are the same"); book 11, chapter 24 ("The divine Trinity in creation"); book 11, chapter 26 ("The partial image of the Trinity in human nature"); book 11, chapter 28 ("Whether we should approximate more nearly to the image of the divine Trinity by loving our love of our existence and our knowledge"); and book 11, chapter 29 ("The angels' knowledge of the Trinity").

——. *Confessions.* Translated by R. S. Pine-Coffin (New York: Penguin, 1961). Cf. Augustine, *Confessions,* translated by J. G. Pilkington, NPNF First Series 1 (Peabody, Mass.: Hendrickson, 1994). Only a few short sections of the *Confessions* directly concern the Trinity, but they are not to be missed. Of particular interest are Augustine's ruminations in book 13, chapter 11. Augustine reminds all theologians that any attempt to comprehend the Trinity's mystery must be rooted in spiritual health and will still fall far short of the truth of the matter. "Who can understand the omnipotent Trinity?" Augustine asks. "We all speak of it, though we may not speak of it as it truly is, for rarely does a soul know what it is saying when it speaks of the Trinity. Men wrangle and dispute about it, but it is a vision that is given to none unless they are at peace. . . . This is a mystery none can explain, and which of us would presume to assert that he can?" (Penguin ed., pp. 318-19).

——. *The Enchiridion; or, On Faith, Hope and Love.* Translated by J. F. Shaw. NPNF First Series 3 (Peabody, Mass.: Hendrickson, 1994). Cf. St. Augustine, *Faith, Hope, and Charity,* translated by Louis A. Arand, ACW 3 (New York: Newman Press, 1947). Consult chapter 3, "The Triune God is the author of all being, but not the cause of evil"; chapter 10, "The God-Man alone redeems our fallen race"; chapter 11, "The Excellency of God's grace becomes manifest through the Incarnation"; and chapter 12, "Christ is not the Son of the Holy Spirit, though He is born of Him. His birth of the Holy Spirit again proclaims the gratuitous character of divine grace." Though the number of passages specifically dealing with trinitarian concerns are relatively limited in Augustine's handbook of the faith, those we discover are gems. Minutes spent mining will prove worthwhile.

———. *Faith and the Creed.* Translated by S. D. F. Salmond. NPNF First Series 3 (Peabody, Mass.: Hendrickson, 1994). Note particularly chapter 3, in which Augustine discusses the Son's designation as the Word, and chapter 4, where Augustine addresses a number of important christological questions with trinitarian implications. In a striking series of assertions, Augustine develops the Son's relationship to the Father and to those to whom he has committed himself in the Incarnation. Chapter 3, "Of the Holy Spirit and the Mystery of the Trinity," is an extremely helpful summary of Augustine's thoughts on the Trinity.

———. *Letters 165-203.* Translated by Sister Wilfrid Parsons, S.N.D. FC 4 (Washington, D.C.: Catholic University of America Press, 1955).

———. *Letters 204-70.* Translated by Sister Wilfrid Parsons, S.N.D. FC 5 (Washington, D.C.: Catholic University of America Press, 1955). Augustine wrote hundreds of letters, many concerning key theological concepts and issues. Among these are scattered a number of significant letters concerning the Trinity and guidelines for trinitarian reflection. Key letters include 170, 174, and 238-42. In letter 170, for instance, Augustine deals with a constellation of key concepts within a few short pages: the deity of the Holy Spirit, the procession of the Spirit, and analogical language in trinitarian reflection. He also concisely exegetes John 14:28 ("the Father is greater than I") and Philippians 2:7 (the Son "made himself nothing").

———. *Of the Morals of the Catholic Church.* Translated by Richard Stothert. NPNF First Series 4 (Peabody, Mass.: Hendrickson, 1994). One of a series of works written by Augustine to combat Manichaeism. Cf. especially chapters 13-14.

———. *On Christian Teaching.* Translated by R. P. H. Green (Oxford and New York: Oxford University Press, 1997). A short work containing seven key propositions concerning the Trinity, ably summarized by Augustine in Book 1.5. Readers convinced that Augustine loses the social reality of the Trinity through the use of abstract or unscriptural language should read this work carefully. In fact, Augustine clearly grounds the unity of God in the Father, rather than in the common essence shared by all three persons.

———. *On the Creed.* Translated by C. L. Cornish. NPNF First Series 3 (Peabody, Mass.: Hendrickson, 1994). A sermon delivered by Augustine to catechumens, filled with trinitarian insights. In section 3, for example, we have a succinct discussion of the "begetting" of the Son and its implication for the Son's relationship to the Father. In the same section Augustine analyzes the will of the Son and the will of the Father, arguing that Father and Son are unified in their will and intentions. "One will of the Father and Son, because one nature. For it is impossible for the will of the Son to be any whit parted from the Father's will. God and God; both one God: Almighty and Almighty; both One Almighty" (p. 370).

———. *On the Merits and Forgiveness of Sins, and On the Baptism of Infants.* Translated by Peter Holmes. NPNF First Series 5 (Peabody, Mass.: Hendrickson, 1994). Augustine links trinitarian thoughts to his understanding of Christ as genuinely divine and human. In Augustine's thoughts on the forgiveness of sin we occasionally discover profound reflection on the relationship between Jesus' divine and human nature and its implication for Christ's body, the church.

———. *On the Soul and Its Origin.* Translated by Peter Holmes. NPNF First Series 5 (Peabody, Mass.: Hendrickson, 1994). Augustine responds to the error of a young theologian who mistakenly argued that the human soul is an emanation from God's own nature. In his reply Augustine reminds all who would think well of the Trinity that God has no "parts." The soul is not a "part" of God. "We do not even say that the Son or the Holy Ghost is a part of God, although we affirm that the Father, the Son, and the Holy Spirit are all of one and the same nature" (Book 2, ch. 5, pp. 332-33).

———. *On the Spirit and the Letter.* Translated by Peter Holmes. NPNF First Series 5 (Peabody, Mass.: Hendrickson, 1994). Augustine affirms the deity of the Spirit, identifying the Holy Spirit with the finger of God who inscribed the ten commandments on the tablets of stone. The finger of God who inscribed the commandments is the same finger who sanctifies the Christian, "in order that, living by faith, we may do good works through love" (ch. 28, p. 95).

———. *Reply to Faustus the Manichaean.* Translated by Richard Stothert. NPNF First Series 4 (Peabody, Mass.: Hendrickson, 1994). Of interest is Augustine's reply to Faustus' inability to imagine "the God of Christians" being "born from the womb." Augustine replies that the "God over all" was born in "that feeble nature which He took of us, that in it He might die for us, and heal it in us." Attention should also be paid to Augustine's extended reply in book 20 to Faustus' assertion that

Manichaean theology was trinitarian. Augustine employs his trinitarian theology to criticize Faustus' attempt to co-opt trinitarian language and models.

———. *Sermons for Christmas and Epiphany.* Translated by Thomas Comerford Lawler. ACW 15 (New York: Newman Press, 1952). Note especially sermon 15, on John 12:44-50. Augustine includes sections on "The Two Births of Christ," "Why Christ is called the true Son of God," "No-one except Christ has dared to say that he is one with the Father," "The Son's equality with the Father," and "The Word of God, the Commandment of the Father."

———. *Sermons on Selected Lessons of the New Testament.* Translated by R. G. MacMullen. NPNF First Series 6 (Peabody, Mass.: Hendrickson, 1994). A series of sermons on New Testament themes, occasionally containing significant comments on the Trinity. Sermons 1-2, 21, 30-31, 38, 41-42, 53, 55, and 67-70 contain the richest trinitarian insights.

———. *The Trinity.* Translated by Edmund Hill, O.P. (Brooklyn: New City Press, 1991). Cf. also Augustine, *On the Trinity,* translated by Arthur West Haddan, NPNF First Series 3 (Peabody, Mass.: Hendrickson, 1994). A key work for understanding the development of trinitarian theology in the Latin tradition and more particularly in the theology of Thomas Aquinas. Augustine perceives the reflection of the Trinity in the inner self as created in God's image: the memory, understanding, and will. Debate continues to rage as to whether Augustine too strongly separates substance from person in his model, with some arguing that he has unwittingly created an impersonal model of the Trinity. Others contend this criticism reflects a poor reading of Augustine and the tendency of an initial error in interpreting Augustine's thought to be passed on like a virus among modern scholars. The jury is still out.

———. "Of the Words of St. Matthew's gospel, ch. 3:13, 'Then Jesus cometh from Galilee to the Jordan unto John, to be baptized of Him.' Concerning the Trinity." Sermon 2 in *Sermons on Selected Lessons of the New Testament* (see above). A great place to start for those who might need an outline of sorts for Augustine's thoughts on the Trinity.

Saint Hilary of Poitiers. *The Trinity.* Translated by Stephen McKenna. FC 25 (Washington, D.C.: Catholic University of America Press, 1954). Cf. also St. Hilary of Poitiers, *On the Trinity,* in *Select Works,* NPNF Second Series 9 (Peabody, Mass.: Hendrickson, 1994). Some consider this the first systematic and scientific study of the Trinity by a Latin writer. Hilary was first exposed to the Nicene *homoousion* during his exile in the East, and both his trinitarian insights and ability to communicate the thinking of the Greek fathers into comprehensible Latin neologisms are quite remarkable. Hilary's treatise on the Trinity has had a lasting effect on the church, with other worthies such as Augustine, Leo, and Aquinas more than willing to draw upon its riches.

Marius Victorinus. *Theological Treatises on the Trinity.* Translated by Mary T. Clark, R.S.C.J. FC 69 (Washington, D.C.: Catholic University of America Press, 1979). Victorinus produced the first Latin work on the Trinity that analyzes the doctrine from a metaphysical perspective. Hence, some readers will find Victorinus too Platonic for their taste. Still, Augustine valued both the man and the work. Victorinus' use of Platonic categories to lay the foundation for the possibility of exploring divine mysteries such as the Trinity is quite intriguing, and his attempt to draw together "the teaching of reason" and the exegesis of Scripture laudable.

————. *Letter of Marius Victorinus, Rhetor of the City of Rome, to Candidus the Arian.* Translated by Mary T. Clark, R.S.C.J. FC 69 (Washington, D.C.: Catholic University of America Press, 1979). The correspondence between Victorinus and the Arian Candidus illustrates well the struggle of the early Christian community to affirm divine attributes such as immutability, and to equally affirm the Father's begetting of the Son. For Arians such as Candidus, the first proposition — God is unchangeable — ruled out the possibility of a genuine generation or begetting of a Son of the same nature. Victorinus defends the possibility of a divine begetting, more or less using his Platonic background to do so.

————. *Against Arius.* Translated by Mary T. Clark, R.S.C.J. FC 69 (Washington: D.C.: Catholic University of America Press, 1979). Victorinus makes his way through the gospels and Paul's epistles, seeing in each a particular trinitarian theme or issue addressed. For example, in his exegesis of Colossians Victorinus focuses on the begetting of the Son and the creation of the intelligible world. If creation itself is the work of Jesus, must he not be God? Mary Clark has also included three other works of Victorinus against Arius in this rich volume.

2. Medieval, Reformation, and Modern Resources

Medieval, Reformation, and Post-Reformation Contributions

Richard of St. Victor, *"Book Three of the Trinity"* in *Richard of St. Victor: The Twelve Patriarchs, The Mystical Ark, Book Three of the Trinity.* Translated by Grover A. Zinn (New York: Paulist Press, 1979), pp. 371-97. Unfortunately, very little of medieval Catholic theologian Richard of St. Victor's writings has been translated into English. Only this portion ("Book Three") of his influential *The Trinity* is translated and available to contemporary English readers. The Victorine explores phenomenologically the meaning of "charity" (love) for human and divine being and concludes that if God is love three equal persons must exist in God: "In order for the charity to be true, it demands a plurality of persons; in order for charity to be perfected, it requires a Trinity of persons" (p. 387). The implication of this and the significance of the book lie in the development of an alternative to the overwhelmingly Augustinian emphasis on the unity of God in Western trinitarian thought. Richard of St. Victor's idea of God as community of persons paved the way for a rediscovery and renewal of Eastern thought about the Trinity and for the twentieth-century social analogy of the Trinity.

William of Auvergne, *The Trinity, Or the First Principle (De trinitate, seu de primo principio).* Translated by Roland J. Teske and Francis C. Wade (Milwaukee: Marquette University Press, 1989). William of Auvergne was appointed bishop of Paris by Pope Gregory IX in 1228 and died in 1249. His treatise on the Trinity stands as one of the great classics of medieval Catholic trinitarian thought. The treatise is the first part of a larger work known as *The Teaching on God in the Mode of Wisdom.* In it one finds a scholastic demonstration of the Christian doctrine of the Trinity that depends heavily on Aristotelian metaphysics. Some scholars find William's metaphysical theology and trinitarian reflections anticipatory of Thomas Aquinas's while others discover significant differences. In any case, William of Auvergne's treatment of the doctrine of the Trinity is completely orthodox and significant only in its appropriation of Aristotelian categories to explain and express Augustinian ideas of the divine triunity. The emphasis in this medieval classic, as in medieval Western theology generally, is on God's unity of being (essence).

Servetus, Michael. "The Two Treatises of Servetus on the Trinity." Translated by Earl Morse Wilbur in *Harvard Theological Studies* (extra number, 1932). The Spanish anti-trinitarian thinker Michael Servetus published two essays against the orthodox doctrine of Trinity which led to his arrest and execution in Geneva in 1553. The two essays translated and published here are "On the Errors of the Trinity" and "Dialogues on the Trinity." It is very difficult to discern exactly what Servetus believed about the Trinity. Clearly he did not believe in three equal and eternal distinct persons who share one substance. He was anti-Nicene. However, he did attempt to develop his own model of the Trinity which combined aspects of several heretical ideas of the Godhead. The significance of these essays and of Servetus' life and "martyrdom" generally lies in their influence on the Socinian movement, which in turn helped give rise to Unitarianism in Britain and North America more than two hundred years later. Socinus believed in the Trinity not as three distinct hypostases of God but as a series of three dispositions of the divine being for different offices. While this sounds modalistic, the Spanish doctor and theologian also taught a kind of subordinationism of the Son and Spirit to the Father. Few, if any, have been able to provide a coherent account of Servetus' possibly confused idea of the Trinity.

Bickersteth, Edward Henry. *The Trinity: Scripture Testimony to the One Eternal Godhead of the Father, and of the Son, and of the Holy Spirit* (Grand Rapids: Kregel Publications, 1959). This volume, earlier published under the title *The Rock of Ages,* was written by an English parson in response to the rise of Unitarianism in England and New England in the nineteenth century. The author engages in detailed, meticulous examination of biblical passages that support the classical doctrine of the Trinity and undermine all forms of unitarian denial of the ontological triunity of God. Although the book lacks any novel or innovative approach or insights, the author clearly did not intend it to provide them. Its value lies primarily in its marshaling of mountains of biblical exegesis to support the doctrine of the Trinity at a time when that doctrine was under severe attack and in decline.

Edwards, Jonathan. "An Essay on the Trinity" in *Jonathan Edwards: Representative Selections.* Edited by Clarence H. Faust and Thomas H. Johnson (New York: American Book Company, 1935), pp. 375-81. This little essay by the great North American Puritan minister and philosopher-theologian Jonathan Edwards is extremely brief but pregnant with insights and implications for the modern renewal of the dogma of the

Trinity. Drawing on Enlightenment idealism, the Puritan divine expresses the triunity in terms of Mind: "The F[ather] is the Deity subsisting in the Prime, unoriginated & most absolute manner, or the deity in its direct existence. The Son is the deity generated by Gods understanding, or having an Idea of himself & subsisting in that Idea. The Holy Gh[ost] is the Deity subsisting in act, or the divine essence flowing out and Breathed forth in Gods Infinite love to & delight in himself. & I believe the whole divine Essence does Truly & distinctly subsist both in the divine Idea & divine Love, and that each of them are Properly distinct Persons" (p. 379). Ironically, Edwards here anticipates Hegel's notion of the Trinity a century later. He admits toward the end of the essay that it leaves the personality of the Holy Spirit undeveloped.

Schleiermacher, Friedrich. "On the Discrepancy Between the Sabellian and Athanasian Method of Representing the Doctrine of the Trinity." Translated by M. Stuart. *The Biblical Repository and Quarterly Observer* 18 (April, 1835): 265-353; and 19, 20 (1835): 1-116. The article here translated and edited for American readers was originally written and published by Friedrich Schleiermacher, the "father of liberal Protestant theology," in the German publication *Theologische Zeitschrift* in 1822. In it the German theologian provided a sympathetic reinterpretation of the trinitarian thought of Sabellius, the third-century North African Christian theologian generally considered by orthodox-catholic Christians a heretic. In this article Schleiermacher demonstrates his own tendency to relativize the consensual creedal tradition of Christian thought insofar as he judges it defective biblically and experientially. Without discarding early Christian orthodox trinitarian thought entirely, he attempts to show that at least some trinitarian thinkers regarded as heretics by the official church of the Constantinian era and later were not as heretical as generally thought. Very little is revealed in this article about Schleiermacher's own views on the Trinity. Nevertheless, the essay stands as an often-forgotten and neglected example of the great liberal theologian's treatment of the history of the doctrine of the Trinity. He clearly did not consider the Athanasian (Nicene) dogma of the Trinity complete in itself, especially insofar as it rejected all the possible alternatives. Schleiermacher relativized the official dogma by placing it within a historical context of concern with Arianism and attempted to show that the trinitarian thought of Sabellius was another option rarely if ever given its due.

Twentieth-Century Renaissance

Barth, Karl. *The Doctrine of the Word of God (Prolegomena to Church Dog-matics). Church Dogmatics I.1.* Translated by G. T. Thomson (New York: Charles Scribner's Sons, 1936). Without doubt or dispute Swiss theolo-gian and father of the "Neo-Orthodox" movement in modern Prot-estant theology Karl Barth is the prime mover of the twentieth-century renaissance of trinitarian thought. The entire multi-volumed *Church Dogmatics* of which this volume is "volume one, part one" is trinitarian in structure. Explorations of God's triunity are scattered throughout all thirteen part-volumes. In this introductory and programmatic volume the author lays out his first principles. Extrapolating from the presup-positions that "God is Lord" and "God speaks" *(Deus dixit),* Barth con-cludes that Father, Son, and Holy Spirit are three eternal and equal *Seinsweisen* ("modes of being") of God. The Trinity is a strict deduction from the reality of God's speech in God's revelation of himself. Barth re-fuses any difference between God himself and God's self-revelation. The reality of divine self-revelation requires recognition that "God Himself in unimpaired unity yet also in unimpaired difference is Revealer, Reve-lation, and Revealedness" (p. 339). By linking Trinity inextricably with revelation Barth helped revive the dogma neglected for several hundred years and especially in the previous century. Critics have charged Barth with crypto-modalism. The influence of Augustine's psychological analogies and emphasis on divine unity is undeniable. Nevertheless, Barth clearly affirmed the three distinct "persons" of God even if he was reluctant to use the term "persons" due to the inevitable individualistic connotations of that word in both modern German and modern En-glish.

Boff, Leonardo. *Trinity and Society.* Translated by Paul Burns (Maryknoll, N.Y.: Orbis Books, 1988). Brazilian Catholic theologian and liberation-ist Boff here presents a liberation theology perspective on the doctrine of the Trinity. The book presents a survey of the historical development of the doctrine and culminates in a chapter (15) entitled "Amen: The Whole Mystery in a Nutshell" that summarizes the classical Christian doctrine of the Trinity and also re-presents the author's practical appli-cation of the Trinity to liberation of humanity: "From the perichoresis-communion of the three divine Persons derive impulses to liberation: of each and every human person, of society, of the church and of the poor, in the double-critical and constructive-sense. *Human beings* are called to rise above all mechanisms of egoism and live their vocation of communion" (p. 236). Boff's model of the Trinity emphasizes community and thus is closest to the so-called "social analogy." Its political implications are drawn out by the Brazilian theologian to emphasize the "image of God" as reflecting trinitarian equality, mutuality, and non-egoism.

Hill, William J. *The Three-Personed God: The Trinity as a Mystery of Salvation.* (Washington, D.C.: Catholic University of America Press, 1982). The title of this book is taken from a prayer and poem by John Donne: "Batter my heart, Three-Personed God." The author, a twentieth-century Catholic theologian, surveys a vast variety of options in twentieth-century trinitarian and pseudo-trinitarian Christian theology with the intention of helping revive and renew the doctrine so neglected in the previous century. He digs deeply into the wells of past tradition and critiques contemporary models of triunity in order to show that the importance of the Trinity doctrine lies in its inseparable connection with the reality of salvation. Both mysteries are about human existence as well as about God's relational love within himself and toward humanity. This book is one of the better critical surveys of modern and contemporary (especially twentieth-century) Catholic and Protestant trinitarian theologies, but it does not break any new ground in or by itself. Its value lies in the insightful survey it provides of others' views.

Hodgson, Leonard. *The Doctrine of the Trinity* (New York: Charles Scribner's Sons, 1944). Leonard Hodgson provides in this little treatise the foundation for the revival of a "social Trinity" or "social analogy" in modern trinitarian thought. Reacting against the rise of various unitarianisms and Sabellianism in modern Christian theology, he argues that "personality" itself requires a plurality of persons in community. The unity of God is not bare mathematical unity, but "internally constitutive unity" consistent with parts constituting a whole. Hodgson also reasons that without this internal multiplicity-in-unity (community) God as personal would require the world as his counterpart, for there can be no such thing as personality without relationship. Although the British theologian believed that his social model of the divine triunity is consistent with Augustine's, Thomas's, and Calvin's models of the Trinity, it is doubtful that most in the Western Christian tradition would have agreed with the stress laid here on the communal nature of the divine being.

Jenson, Robert W. *The Triune Identity: God According to the Gospel* (Philadelphia: Fortress Press, 1982). This volume represents an extension of the reflections on Barth's doctrine of the Trinity begun in the author's earlier work, *God After God*. Lutheran theologian Jenson agrees with the theologians of hope and eschatology, Moltmann and Pannenberg, that God cannot be separated from time and history. He also disagrees with process theology that God evolves. The solution is to recognize God as a "triune infinity" eventfulness and all-encompassing being and power. The author's subtlety and willingness to embrace and affirm paradox is revealed in this summary statement: "The temporal infinity that opens before us and so surrounds us is the inexhaustibility of one event, the final appropriation of all history by the particular love actual as Jesus of Nazareth" (p. 176). *The Triune Identity* gives rise to at least as many questions as it answers, which is not bad so long as readers know it as they embark on this voyage.

Jüngel, Eberhard. *The Doctrine of the Trinity: God's Being Is in Becoming* (Grand Rapids: Eerdmans, 1976). This little volume was originally published in Germany and quickly became a widely discussed commentary on Barth's doctrine of God as trinitarian being with a history. According to the Tübingen Protestant theologian, Barth's doctrine of the Trinity implies more than many have seen in it. God's being is not static essence (immanent Trinity apart from historicity) but historical becoming. This "becoming," however, is not change but unfolding through self-expression and self-interpretation, especially on the cross of Jesus Christ which most clearly reveals the triune struggle of God within himself in world history. The author's thought about God and time, triunity and becoming, is extremely subtle, dialectical, and open to varying interpretations. The thesis is that the suffering of Jesus Christ on the cross was not merely an outward event that left the inner-trinitarian being of God untouched, but an inner-trinitarian event in which God *as God* identifies himself with the crucified Jesus. The author clearly does not intend a "process" view of God in which God evolves. Rather, God actualizes himself as who he is in and through the salvation-historical events such as the cross and resurrection of Jesus, which impact God's eternity.

————. *God as the Mystery of the World: On the Foundation of the Theology of the Crucified One in the Dispute Between Theism and Atheism*. Translated by Darrell L. Guder (Grand Rapids: Eerdmans, 1983). Widely considered both one of the most profound and one of the most provocative treatises on the doctrine of God in contemporary theology, this extremely challenging book declares and argues that in the death of Jesus Christ on the cross God becomes God. That is, God is constituted as who he is in the self-chosen suffering and death of Jesus. This is a direct challenge to classical Christian theism, which the author considers more philosophical than truly Christian. If God is love, then God and death come together in Christ and his cross. The crucified Jesus is the primary "vestige of the Trinity" and Father, Son, and Holy Spirit are both distinguished and united as "one God" in this cross event that takes death into God's own life and unleashes God's powerful, kenotic love into human history. *God as the Mystery of the World* is enigmatic, almost mystical. It is certainly dialectical and anti-natural theology and rationalism. The God of Jesus and therefore of Christians is a crucified God and not at all the passionless, immutable God of classical theism.

Kasper, Walter. *The God of Jesus Christ.* Translated by Matthew J. O'Connell (New York: Crossroad, 1984). Although not a treatise on the Trinity per se, *The God of Jesus Christ* contains an entire section (Part Three) on "The Trinitarian Mystery of God." The author is an influential German Catholic theologian and bishop who seeks to chart out a middle ground between Catholic traditionalism and modernism. He argues that the trinitarian confession (Nicene with contemporary elucidations) is the answer to modern atheism, which rejects a different God than the triune God of Jesus Christ. In this book the German bishop presents what is widely considered the most profound and correct interpretation of the controversial "Rahner's Rule" regarding the immanent and economic Trinity. According to Kasper, the great Austrian Catholic theologian meant that the economic Trinity reveals the immanent Trinity authentically and that the immanent triune life of God is lived out in the economy of salvation history without being dissolved in time and change.

LaCugna, Catherine Mowry. *God for Us: The Trinity and Christian Life* (San Francisco: HarperSanFrancisco, 1991). Catholic theologian LaCugna here presents an original treatise on the Trinity that connects it with salvation in the broadest sense. According to her, the Trinity is not a mystery of speculation ("cosmic numerology") but an expression of the involvement of God in redemptive life. She explores the history of the doctrine in the Cappadocian fathers, Augustine, Thomas Aquinas, and Gregory Palamas and argues that the inner meaning of the Trinity in all of these has more to do with salvation history and experience than with theistic speculation. LaCugna focuses on the economic Trinity and es-chews speculation into the immanent Trinity without denying its reality altogether. She demonstrates that "The doctrine of the Trinity is ulti-mately . . . a teaching not about the abstract nature of God, nor about God in isolation from everything other than God, but a teaching about God's life with us and our life with each other" (p. 1).

Lampe, G. W. H. *God as Spirit* (Oxford: Clarendon Press, 1977). British theologian Geoffrey Lampe argues that the classical, orthodox doctrine of the Trinity is mistaken because Christian scripture and experience re-veal no ontological distinction between any "person" of God and "Spirit." Spirit is the deity of Jesus Christ ("Spirit Christology" in prefer-ence to "Logos Christology"); Spirit is God himself; Spirit is the divine activity and presence. God is Spirit. Jesus Christ is God because he is full of the Spirit. There are not three "persons" of God but only one ex-pressed in varying ways. Lampe verges on unitarianism or at least Sabellianism. He concludes by saying "I believe that the Trinitarian model is in the end less satisfactory for the articulation of our basic Christian experience than the unifying concept of God as Spirit" (p. 228). This volume stands as an interesting, if heretical, counterpoint to the twentieth-century renaissance of the doctrine of the Trinity. Its basic thrust is much closer to that of the nineteenth-century liberal neglect or even rejection of the doctrine of the Trinity.

Lee, Jung Young. *The Trinity in Asian Perspective* (Nashville: Abingdon Press, 1996). Korean Christian theologian Lee provides an Asian cultural per-spective on the doctrine of the Trinity that is meant to complement and supplement rather than replace Western perspectives. Among other things this means emphasizing the familial image of the Trinity rooted in Asian patterns of family relationships. The author suggests that for an Asian, no family is complete without both the father-son (or father-child) relation and the mother-child relation. Therefore, the Holy Spirit (within a Confucian perspective) might be imagined as the Mother from whom the divine Son proceeds. This book provides a much-needed corrective to the heavily Augustinian and Western European domination of trinitarian thought without escaping from all Western concepts.

Moltmann, Jürgen. *The Trinity and the Kingdom: The Doctrine of God.* Translated by Margaret Kohl (San Francisco: Harper & Row, 1981). Moltmann is widely considered one of the most important and controversial trinitarian theologians of the twentieth century. Largely due to the constructive trinitarian theology of this volume he has been accused of tritheism. According to *The Trinity and the Kingdom* (only one of several books in which the author deals with the Trinity), God's economic trinitarian being is his immanent trinitarian being and vice versa. God's trinitarian being is identical with the processes and patterns of the Kingdom of God in world history. Only in the end of history will the immanent Trinity appear, and there is some sense in which God is already "there." However, in this particular volume, the founder of the so-called "theology of hope" wishes to emphasize the openness of God as Trinity for the world and for history. Through the sending of the Son who is none other than Jesus and through the mission of the Spirit, God constitutes himself together with his Kingdom. The history of the Kingdom of God and of God himself cannot be divided. The author claims that the unity of God as perfect harmony between Father, Son, and Spirit is eschatological — a unity of goal rather than of origin. This leads some critics to charge him with the heresy of tritheism.

O'Donnell, John J. *Trinity and Temporality: The Christian Doctrine of God in the Light of Process Theology and the Theology of Hope* (New York: Oxford University Press, 1983). O'Donnell's comparative study of two twentieth-century theologies — process theology and German theologian Moltmann's trinitarian theology of the cross — leads to the conclusion that contemporary Christian theology is radically revising classical theism, especially in the area of God's relationship with time. According to the author, God is no longer being understood in terms of pure "being" but now more and more in terms of "becoming." After a careful critical examination of process theology's panentheistic view of God in which God and the world are inseparably related and mutually enriching, the author turns to the so-called "theology of hope" worked out by Moltmann in which God's self-limiting involvement with the world is the basis of God's temporality. The God/world relationship is structured in a trinitarian fashion in which God's economic history with the world has a real (ontological) impact on his immanent being. The sending of the Son of God as Jesus of Nazareth is not merely a process outside of God but an event in the life of God. For Moltmann (and for O'Donnell) the incarnation implies that God is not "one divine nature" or "one absolute subject" but a community with a history open to the world.

145

Panikkar, Raimundo. *The Trinity and the Religious Experience of Man: Icon-Person-Mystery* (New York: Orbis Books, 1973). Written by a Christian scholar of Eastern religions, this book explores the similarities between concepts of God in the latter and the Christian doctrine of the Trinity. Panikkar's thesis, defended throughout the volume, is that "It is simply an unwarranted overstatement to affirm that the trinitarian conception of the Ultimate, and with it of the whole of reality, is an exclusive Christian insight or revelation" (p. viii). He considers the Trinity to be a concept found in some form throughout the world's great religions — a "junction where the authentic spiritual dimensions of all religions meet" (p. 42). A Christian theologian steeped in orthodox, Nicene trinitarianism (especially the social trinitarianism of the Cappadocians and Richard of St. Victor) may find Panikkar's discoveries of correspondences between, for example, the "brahman" of the Upanishadic traditions of India (e.g., *advaita Vedanta*) and the Christian dogma of the Trinity forced if not heretical. Nevertheless, the author breaks new ground in world religions dialogue in this and other writings.

Peters, Ted. *God as Trinity: Relationality and Temporality in Divine Life* (Louisville: Westminster/John Knox Press, 1993). This book is a particularly lucid analysis and critical evaluation of twentieth-century trinitarian thought by an influential Lutheran theologian. The author provides stimulating and occasionally controversial explanations and critiques of leading trinitarian thinkers such as German theologians Moltmann and Pannenberg. Peters's orientation in theology is closest to theirs (so-called "theology of hope" or "eschatological theology"), and he provides his own suggestions about the relationship between Trinity and history/eschatology. Among other theses set forth and defended ably by the author is "To understand God as Trinity in the economy of salvation requires that God be both temporal and eternal" (p. 173). For Peters the immanent Trinity is eschatological while the economic Trinity is historical. Yet, the two are not to be divided. The key to this conceptuality lies in the concept of "temporal holism." Readers seeking a well-written, lucid, accurate survey of twentieth-century trinitarianism with some critical and constructive modifications of leading trinitarian thinkers can find no better work written in the last decade of the century than this one.

Pittenger, Norman. *The Divine Triunity* (Philadelphia: United Church Press, 1977). British process theologian Norman Pittenger strove mightily to

146

provide a process-theological interpretation of the doctrine of the Trinity: God as everlasting creative agency who works everywhere, God as self-expressive Word, and God as responsive agency. In the end, in spite of attempts to avoid it, the best Pittenger can provide is a modalistic interpretation of the Trinity that falls far short of three distinct subsistences (persons) in God. Finally, he concludes that the doctrine of the Trinity really functions to represent a human hope and experience: "The belief that God is triune maintains for us the wonder and glory of the divine, guarantees for us that both personality and sociality are grounded in the way things go in the world, and opens to our minds and hearts the cosmic Love which creates us, which discloses itself to us, and which through our own response (however imperfect and feeble) enriches our lives — and adds joy to the being of God himself" (pp. 117-18).

Pohle, Joseph. *The Divine Trinity: A Dogmatic Treatise.* Translated by Arthur Preuss (St. Louis: B. Herder, 1911). A standard Roman Catholic explication and defense of the orthodox doctrine of the Trinity by a German Catholic theologian soon after the beginning of the twentieth century. The book begins with a prolegomenon entitled "Introductory Remarks" that includes a strong emphasis on the *de Deo uno* (one God). In truly Augustinian-Thomist fashion the author states that "Unity, simplicity, and unicity are as essential to the mystery of the blessed Trinity as the concept of triunity itself" (2). Such a statement, placed at the very beginning of a dogmatic treatise on the Trinity, invites strong reaction from trinitarian thinkers in the second half of the twentieth century. Karl Rahner, perhaps the most influential Catholic theologian since Thomas Aquinas, criticized this approach which tended to make the triunity of God secondary to God's unity and simplicity. Pohle's volume includes biblical and historical materials supporting the classical Augustinian-Thomist doctrine of the Trinity and rejects as heresy the "Greek schism," including the Eastern Orthodox denial of the *filioque* (procession of the Holy Spirit from both Father and Son). The book concludes with defenses of the Catholic doctrines of the unity of all external operations of the three divine persons *(omnia opera trinitatis ad extra indivisa sunt)* and "perichoresis" (mutual inexistence of the three). Overall, Pohle's dogmatic treatise is a classic of Catholic scholastic trinitarian thought.

Rahner, Karl. *The Trinity* (New York: Herder and Herder, 1970). In this little book, perhaps the most influential Roman Catholic theologian since

Thomas Aquinas criticizes most Western Christians for being little more than "mere monotheists." He argues that the doctrine of the Trinity could be dropped from the Christian consciousness and little about Christian literature would change. He wanted to change this situation by demonstrating the intimate connection between trinitarian dogma and reflection and Christian salvation and life. Two proposals of Rahner's have become the subjects of great dispute as well as constructive discussion. The Austrian theologian agreed with Karl Barth that "person" is problematic for referring to the three distinctions within God due to the term's inevitable individualistic connotations. He suggested "distinct manner of subsisting" as a theological (not popular) translation for "hypostasis." Second, Rahner here provides the principle — known later as "Rahner's Rule" — that *the economic Trinity is the immanent Trinity and the immanent Trinity is the economic Trinity.* In other words, there is no disjunction between God-in-himself and God-for-us. The activity of the three persons in salvation history is God himself in action for us and among us. This rule or principle gave rise to numerous doctoral dissertations, scholarly articles, and books after the publication of *The Trinity.* Some critics accused Rahner of melting God into history. Others hailed his insight as a cornerstone of trinitarian renewal. In any case, Rahner's little book helped stimulate new thinking about the Trinity in twentieth-century Christian theology.

Richardson, Cyril C. *The Doctrine of the Trinity* (New York and Nashville: Abingdon Press, 1958). British biblical scholar and systematic theologian Richardson criticizes the orthodox doctrine of the Trinity in this little volume supportive of a modalistic model of God. "The 'threeness' of the Trinity is an arbitrary and unpersuasive doctrine" (p. 111). Instead of thinking of God as three distinct persons, the author argues, we should regard Father, Son, and Holy Spirit as three aspects of God in his relations with us (p. 112). The author appeals to Friedrich Schleiermacher's revisionist treatment of Sabellius and Sabellianism as support for his rehabilitation of that allegedly heretical model of the Trinity. This little book represents something of a reaction against the rise of the "social analogy" for the Trinity (a revival of interest in the Cappadocians' and Richard of St. Victor's concepts of the three-personed Godhead of love) in mid-twentieth-century British Protestant thought (e.g., Leonard Hodgson).

Torrance, Thomas F. *The Trinitarian Faith: The Evangelical Theology of the*

Ancient Catholic Church (Edinburgh: T. & T. Clark, 1988). The author of these Warfield Lectures (Princeton Theological Seminary, 1981) is widely considered one of the most important Protestant theologians of the second half of the twentieth century as well as a very influential interpreter of the theology of Karl Barth. Torrance has written several books on the doctrine of the Trinity, and this one represents the best of his historical and ecumenical thought on the subject. The book contains reflections on the Niceno-Constantinopolitan Creed (Nicene Creed for short) of 381 A.D. and its implications for understanding Christian faith in the contemporary world as both "catholic" and "evangelical." Torrance's thesis is that the seemingly technical language of the Creed and of the doctrine of the Trinity contained in it and implied by it (e.g., the all-important distinction between "ousia" and "hypostasis") is intrinsically bound up with the gospel of grace itself and with the unity of the church and Christian faith. Thus, the struggles over it throughout the fourth century were not products of speculation or rationalization but rather results of different visions of salvation and church. Torrance here defends the church's triune vision of God as expressed in the language of the Creed and as explained by the fathers of the undivided church (Athanasius, the Cappadocians, et al.) against heretics by demonstrating the "inner logic" of Christian faith that drove it. This volume is one of the finest brief accounts of the story of the development of the Creed and the doctrine of the Trinity throughout the fourth century.

Welch, Claude. *In This Name: The Doctrine of the Trinity in Contemporary Theology* (New York: Charles Scribner's Sons, 1952). *In This Name* is widely regarded as a classic of twentieth-century theology. The author, a highly regarded historical theologian, based this book on his doctoral dissertation at Yale University. It is a critical survey of modern Christian (mostly Protestant) thinking about the Trinity from its neglect in the nineteenth century to its revival in the twentieth. Among the book's outstanding contributions are its critical assessments of the revival of the so-called "social analogy" (e.g., Leonard Hodgson's work on the Trinity) in the twentieth century (especially in Great Britain) and of the renaissance of trinitarian theology in Karl Barth's theology. Welch affirms and defends Barth's preference for "modes of being" over "persons" for the triune distinctions of Father, Son, and Holy Spirit while cautioning that these "are not merely ways of God's being in relation to man, but *God's ways of being God*" (p. 277). This volume represents an important American contribution to the twentieth-century renewal of the doctrine of the Trinity as well as an important critical affirmation of the so-called "psychological analogy" implicit in Barth's own Augustinian-inspired trinitarian theology.

Zizioulas, John D. *Being As Communion: Studies in Personhood and the Church* (Crestwood, N.Y.: St. Vladimir's Press, 1985). This book represents one of the most important works on the Trinity in English in the late twentieth century from an Eastern Orthodox perspective. Any reader in search of an Orthodox and contemporary volume of trinitarian theology cannot do better than peruse this volume. The author explores the connections between "being" (ontology) and "community" or "communion" between persons in trinitarian thought and concludes that an "ontology of personhood" that focuses on relationality arises out of Christian revelation, especially as that bears on the triune being of God. This is a sweeping volume that ranges over a number of related loci of theology: God, Jesus Christ, humanity, church, etc. The author finds the point of connection in the orthodox doctrine of the Trinity.

Index